Marketing Inside

Marketing Inside

How the World's Leading Brands
Structure for Agility, Creativity,
and Impact

Greg Paull

www.amplifypublishing.com

Marketing Inside: How the World's Leading Brands Structure for Agility, Creativity, and Impact

For more information, please contact:
Amplify Publishing, an imprint of Amplify Publishing Group
620 Herndon Parkway, Suite 220
Herndon, VA 20170
info@amplifypublishing.com

Library of Congress Control Number: 2025915612
CPSIA Code: PRV1025A
ISBN-13: 979-8-89138-920-5

Printed in the United States

Contents

Introduction

I was born lucky.

I was born in a country called "The Lucky Country" (Australia) as a native English speaker and to an upper-middle-class family.

I was a curious kid. From age six, I started making Airfix kits, trying to piece together planes, tanks, cars, and other things from the pieces. That sense of logic and planning came in handy in later life and also served as a theme for the cover of this book.

I went to a good school, got exposed to global trends and influences, and by the time I started my first job, I of course thought I knew everything there was to know about marketing.

My first boss told me, "The secret to marketing is honesty—and once you can fake that, you're on your way."

I was always curious to learn more about marketing. In Australia, we had an incredible program called AWARD School, where two nights a week, young prospects would spend three hours with some of the smartest seniors in the business learning about creativity. I thought I, too, could be a copywriter. Over a hundred participants competed and tested their skills. I came in second. You don't win silver; you lose gold. I still remember that someone called David Droga became the top student. I wonder what happened to him.

I spent sixteen years supporting marketers, working for advertising agencies in Australia, Asia, London, and New York. I was again lucky to work on some of the biggest brands and opportunities. In 1994, I sat down with three Finns in Hong Kong as they talked about this strange brand called Nokia for the first time. Ten years later, we had helped that firm become the largest company in Europe, until it lost its way to Apple and inside Microsoft. I got excited by the rush of marketing driving business. I got excited by continuous improvement.

In 2002, I launched Asia's first independent advisor to marketers, R3. Despite our location, our mindset was always to understand and get involved in global marketing. We were lucky again—one of our first clients was Coca-Cola in Atlanta, who at that time still didn't have a robust process to assess its outsourced agency performance. They taught us a lot. We still work with Coca-Cola today.

Our approach was simple—the CEO can turn to McKinsey, Bain, and Boston Consulting Group. The CFO has KPMG, Deloitte, PwC, and EY. The CTO has Gartner. Who does the CMO have as a truly trusted advisor?

We wanted to become "The McKinsey of Marketing."

Even Tiger Woods hires a coach.

We told clients, "We are going to be one of your smallest but most influential partners."

We were very lucky again.

Now we had a front-row seat to watch how marketing was transforming—and we never had to make a single ad.

I still remember that at the Beijing Olympics in 2008, Coca-Cola conducted an incredible torch relay where one hundred million (not a typo) Chinese consumers got personal samples of its product at more than two hundred on-ground events across the country. We were there when Unilever decided to totally change its agency model and become one of the first to reward the best agencies for the best work. During the COVID-19 pandemic, we were alongside Nike as it found new global media partners for the first time in its history.

Through it all, we were lucky to also spend a lot of time with agencies—meeting the greats like Sir Martin Sorrell, John Wren, Al Golin, Jeff Goodby, Maurice Saatchi, Maurice Levy, Arthur Sadoun . . . and god, I wish there were more women on this list because they have an emotional intelligence quotient (EQ) for this industry just unmatched by men. We created the Global Agency Family Tree in 2013, and still to this day, some people think that's pretty much all we do.

Contributors

Just as importantly, we've been side by side with some incredible marketers—ten of whom kindly gave up their time to contribute to this book.

I first met **Shakir Moin** in 2002 when he was just a brand manager at Coca-Cola in Southeast Asia. Even then, he was the most curious, most passionate, and most thoughtful marketer I had met. No wonder he has moved to Atlanta, then Shanghai, and then back to Atlanta. Shakir just wants to spend every minute of his time learning and improving. Come back in five years and check his CV; I am sure you will get goosebumps.

Ed Bell hired us in 2006 (it seems so long ago!) in China when he was working at adidas, because he truly believed (then and now) in seeking independent, well-researched benchmarks. In his role leading marketing globally for Cathay Pacific, he never wanted to do the best work in Hong Kong, or Asia, for that matter—he wants to do only world-class work. Meanwhile, I hate him for speaking fluent Mandarin and Cantonese.

At that same time in those China days, I also got to know **Asmita Dubey** in Shanghai, when she was leading some of WPP's largest media clients. It was already clear to me that she thought differently—she thought way beyond media and was always looking for ways to achieve best practice. Few people have done more to lead a revolution at L'Oréal more than she has.

Emily Ketchen is a rare treasure. A true "third-culture kid" who grew up in so many places, she also spent a good chunk of time in agencies. All this gives her a unique perspective at Lenovo on what global marketing actually is and how to truly work with partners in an open and collaborative way. She thinks differently about her team, about training, about AI, and about learning compared to 99 percent of the marketers I meet. Yes, truly a rare treasure.

Colin Westcott-Pitt has had an incredible career across so many continents but always with one core foundation: "How can we improve?" Imagine a Brit selling Dutch beer to Americans—or across Africa. Now at Glanbia, he's truly found his niche in one of the most entrepreneurial consumer packaged goods (CPG) companies doing truly breakthrough marketing. He's thoughtful, detailed, and inspiring.

These five people all share a common trait: They gave up the comforts of home and went out (just as I did) to explore the broader world of global marketing. They took the risks and reaped the rewards.

Without naming names, I've come to see that there are two types of CMOs in this world. Firstly, the so-called Vanity CMOs—you will see them sipping rosé at the MediaLink event in Cannes or getting a winter break at CES. They will be drinking the Kool-Aid at Mountain View or Menlo Park. They have the VIP seats at the Super Bowl or at the Oscars. Their twenty years of experience might have to cover ten different companies—because sometimes it's hard to hit a moving target. They need to keep finding the next job. Recruiters are their absolute best friends.

Then there are what I would call the Working CMOs—the ones who love the grind, who want to keep learning, who want to truly find out if marketing is getting results. I love me some Working CMO.

You won't get two more boring CVs than **Eric Lempel** of Sony PlayStation and **Cheryl Guerin** of Mastercard. Both have twenty-five-plus years in the same company, and both are true Working Marketers focused on outcomes.

I have probably been involved in five hundred agency pitches at R3, and Eric is the only marketing leader that *really* paid agencies to participate (in 2018) as he sought out creativity for PlayStation. The fact that he appointed a lead agency in London (adamandeveDDB) when his whole marketing team was based in San Francisco speaks to how highly he values creative thinking. All the success of the PlayStation 5 launch is based on this bravery.

Cheryl Guerin has been a critical part of a complete revolution in marketing at Mastercard. The company was one of the first to embrace experiences—and migrate precious media dollars to a far more diverse approach. During her time there, the stock went public at $5. It's now sitting at $570. The brand is firmly in the Interbrand Top Ten, and she has built an amazing team to keep business moving.

What **Tamara Rogers** and her team are doing at Haleon will be studied in marketing textbooks for years to come. Spun off from GSK, Haleon has a plethora of brands and challenging markets, and Tamara has proven her way by engaging her CEO (himself an ex-marketer) and establishing the true value of return on investment (ROI). She and her team are also the most delightful group we've engaged with in recent years—absolute professionalism at the highest level.

It takes a lot of guts to be a market leader and decide to change things. But **Mike Tripp** and his team at the US's number one car brand, Toyota, have done just that. We were so fortunate to be there recently to look at how 350 marketing people can be more efficient, effective, creative, and accountable. In many ways, his bravery to bring us in is the inspiration for this book.

This brings us to **Mukul Deoras** at Colgate—the most unassuming, humble, "under the radar" marketer I have worked with but equally the most thoughtful, passionate, and driven brand ambassador. This is the second book he has been kind enough to help me with. A week doesn't go by where I don't steal this quote from him in 2018: "It's not the learning curve we need for modern marketing—it's the unlearning curve." He remains the most impressive person I know in this industry—and he's equally impressive on cricket knowledge.

Gary Player, a famous golfer, once said, "The harder I work, the luckier I get." Sometimes at R3, it feels like being a duck on the water—gracefully paddling while swimming like mad underneath—the sausage making of marketing consulting sounds easy, but as the demands grow, the workload only gets more intense. Should this marketer be hubbing services? Is the agency serving up its best talent for this client? Have we satisfied the needs of procurement?

Is the MSA between the client and agency world class? Will each country get the partners they are expecting? Are the media rates competitive versus benchmark? And how about the use of generative AI? We can't go a whole day in marketing anymore without mentioning gen AI.

Through all this hard work over the years, one thing has always struck me:

Too many marketers outsource marketing.

It's like that old (bad) joke: "Marketers use agencies like a drunk man uses a lamp post—more for support than illumination."

What's the first thing a CMO typically does when they arrive at a new company? Agency pitch.

What do they do after a year of poor business results? Agency pitch.

What do they do when they need to find influencers? Agency pitch.

What do they do when they are short of ideas? Agency pitch.

I'll never forget when a local marketer in China wanted to put us on an annual retainer. *How lucky*, I thought. What would the scope be? "Well, we will probably run ten pitches this year. We thought it best if you're here to help all of them." We did not end up signing that retainer.

It's time that marketers looked inside. This is the reason this book exists.

Actually, it exists for two reasons—"Marketing Inside" but also "Marketing Inside."

Let me explain . . .

1. **"Marketing Inside" means making marketing count inside the company.**
   Marketing needs to get back into the executive suite and boardroom. It's important. It's the engine for growth. As Mukul Deoras of Colgate tells it, "Marketing has to be the day job of a very senior person in the organization."

   Last year, we ran an important creative review for a global French $20 billion CPG company. The CEO of the company decided he needed to attend every session. Yes, the CEO. He decided that marketing was part of his day job. Of course, he became the magnet that brought in the regional general managers, the COO, the chief growth officers, and, of course, the CMO's team and procurement. In that pitch, a decision was made so quickly in that room, with him leading discussions, that it would make your head spin. A company famous for being misaligned and promiscuous with its decision process suddenly had a real global alignment. The new work speaks for itself—world-class, Cannes-awarded, results-driven marketing.

This CEO put Marketing Inside.

Most people reading this book probably watched the television drama series *Mad Men*—and you'll recall that Don Draper is rarely presenting to the marketing procurement director. He's not talking to the CMO or marketing manager. He's talking to the CEOs of his potential clients—because there once was a time when marketing was onside the C-suite of every Fortune 500 company.

I recently read a biography of Dwight D. Eisenhower, who, as a little-known fact, actually golfed more than any president in history—yes, including *that* president. More than eight hundred times in eight years. What was interesting was more *who* he was golfing with—the CEOs of industry but including the CEO of Young & Rubicam, one of the largest advertising agencies at the time. Creativity mattered then. It should matter again today.

Eisenhower believed in the power of marketing.

I remember working on a project with Omnicom and meeting Monica Shaffer Karo, now the chief client officer at OMD. Since she had previously serviced the Apple account, I asked her innocently, "You know, in all your time servicing Apple, did you ever get the chance to meet Steve Jobs?" I will never forget her answer: "Yes, every Wednesday at twelve o'clock." Steve Jobs, the CEO of what is now a $3 trillion company, would meet with his agency every week to get decisions made and get things moving.

Steve Jobs believed in Marketing Inside.

2. **"Marketing Inside" means optimizing people, processes, and partners to drive the best business outcomes.**

Marketing needs to be more efficient and effective. It's in danger of becoming too tactical, too formulaic, too fragmented, too "not invented here" syndrome, and too awash in not-useful-enough data.

Shakir Moin, the CMO of Coca-Cola North America, said it best: "We want to be a 'learn-it-all' organization, not a 'know-it-all' organization." This year, three hundred Coca-Cola marketers watched the Tom Hanks movie *Apollo 13*—not as a nice "break" from their day jobs but as a stimulant to make them more productive thinkers in their day job. You might remember that the movie is based on the actual Apollo 13 flight, which went through so much engine trouble that the crew on board and the whole of NASA in Houston had to get creative.

Too many marketers have forgotten the importance of being creative.

Likewise, creativity is not a role to be outsourced—it's something marketers need to be actively involved in. Mars ran a global pitch in 2009 for a new brand launch, and they invited one small, scrappy agency, Chris Clarke's Nitro. Chris has a longtime partnership with Mars and wanted his agency to put its best foot forward. So he asked, "Is it OK if we come sit in your office for a week?" The CMO of course agreed, and by the end of Monday, they had some strategic thinking to share with her. By Wednesday, she was already seeing creative ideas in real time. By Friday, she thought *she* had written the ad, so closely was she and her team collaborating.

Here, creativity was brought inside.

We want this book to be a wake-up call to the marketing industry.

Marketing will always be the engine of growth for any company. While the industry has changed more in the last decade than in the previous hundred years, marketing still needs to be the burning platform and the clarion call for a company to look to for growth. Marketing needs to be inside for growth. At the same time, marketers need to retool their insides for growth.

Goosebumps

When Shakir Moin was made US CMO of Coca-Cola, it was the next step in a thirty-year journey for the CPG company that had seen him work all over the world, including some of the most challenging markets possible. The first thing he did was not fire his agency or launch a new marketing tactic; he instead formed a task force of the four marketing heads of each division and himself.

Now, these heads actually had less in common than you might think. Sure, they worked for the same company, but silos had reigned supreme, as in a lot of other companies. For Coca-Cola sparkling to grow, it can of course steal share from Pepsi but potentially also from Powerade and Dasani. They often worked as four independent fiefdoms in a large matrix organization. Now, under Shakir's leadership, they met every fourteen days as a group. And that group's name was . . . "the Goosebumps."

He called them the Goosebumps.

He insisted they share their creative work with each other (something the company had never actively done before) and that all five of them commented on whether they felt . . . goosebumps. But it didn't stop there—they were asked to bring in ideas every two weeks of any work that caused . . . goosebumps. Suddenly ideas were coming from everywhere. The level of cooperation among otherwise disparate teams was never greater.

In 1997, Steve Jobs returned famously to Apple. The first thing he did was call in Jay Chiat from his longtime agency partner TBWA/Chiat Day and develop new advertising. The spot, narrated by Richard Dreyfus, is as fresh today as it ever was:

Here's to the crazy ones, the misfits, the rebels, the troublemakers, the round pegs in the square holes . . . the ones who see things differently—they're not fond of rules . . . You can quote them, disagree with them, glorify or vilify them, but the only thing you can't do is ignore them because they change things . . . they push the human race forward, and while some may see them as the crazy ones, we see genius, because the ones who are crazy enough to think that they can change the world, are the ones who do.

Goosebumps.

At the end of the film *Oppenheimer,* Cillian Murphy approaches Tom Conti, who played Albert Einstein. Oppenheimer states, "When I came to you with those calculations, we thought we might start a chain reaction that might destroy the entire world." To which Einstein replies, "What of it?" Oppenheimer responds, "I believe we did."

Goosebumps.

I was thinking of renaming this book *The Road to Goosebumps*—because without taking the journey that Coca-Cola and others are on, marketing is likely to get crushed.

This all reminded me of an impassioned speech Mastercard's CMO, Raja Rajamannar, has made over the years for the role of experiences: "When six hundred million people are blocking your ads, are actually paying for software or a more expensive subscription to say 'No—I do NOT want to see your advertising!'—then the role of marketing just has to change."

This is the moment for the role of marketing to change.

This is the moment for Marketing Inside.

And I feel lucky just to be a part of it.

Chapter 1
The Evolution of the Marketing Organization

In 2021, Coca-Cola initiated a bold transformation of its global marketing structure by partnering with WPP to create a bespoke agency model known as OpenX. The move marked a fundamental shift in how the company approached its creative and media operations, born out of the need for greater integration, efficiency, and a stronger internal marketing ethos.

But this was *not* an agency move first and foremost.

This was "Marketing Inside."

Coca-Cola's marketing had long operated as a fragmented ecosystem, with different brands and regions functioning like isolated fiefdoms. Shakir Moin, then CMO of Coca-Cola China, and others recognized the need for unity.

Coca-Cola was brave enough to reshape its global operating model. In past years, people in the company would be *promoted* for making advertising. It was the classic "let a thousand flowers bloom." But under the new approach, a series of operating units (OUs) were established to make advertising in nine places, not ninety.

OpenX was the next logical step. Structurally, Coca-Cola reorganized its marketing under a unified model with WPP, consolidating creative, media, data, and strategy into one global team. WPP, in turn, developed a custom agency network with dedicated talent aligned to Coca-Cola's business goals. This was more than a partnership; it was a structural overhaul.

The announcement was made with clarity and ambition. Coca-Cola publicly framed the OpenX launch as a move toward agility, better creativity, and effectiveness across its massive brand portfolio. Industry press picked up the story quickly, and marketers worldwide took notice.

The market response was largely positive. Many saw it as a necessary correction to years of siloed marketing. Internally, Coca-Cola's marketers felt empowered, as the new model brought discipline and inspiration back inside the organization. The result? Marketing was no longer an outsourced function but a collaborative engine of growth.

Coca-Cola didn't just hire a new agency—it rewired how marketing worked from the inside out.

Why Marketing Organizational Restructures Happen

Marketing organizational restructures don't happen by accident—they're a strategic response to evolving business needs, shifting consumer behavior, and the constant demand for greater effectiveness and efficiency. At the core, these restructures are about one thing: growth.

Take Procter & Gamble (P&G), for example. As one of the world's largest advertisers, P&G restructured its marketing organization to cut complexity and drive faster decision-making. In 2019, the company moved away from traditional brand management to a "brand entrepreneurship" model. This meant fewer layers, more direct accountability, and integrated teams with end-to-end responsibility for each brand. The goal wasn't just to reduce costs—it was to accelerate innovation and make marketers more accountable for business results. With billions in media spend at stake, P&G had to ensure that its marketing organization could move at the speed of culture.

Ferrari offers a very different but equally insightful case. Known for exclusivity and craftsmanship, Ferrari faced a new challenge: how to evolve

Coca-Cola

Goal:
Integration,
efficiency & internal
empowerment

Wasn't "hire a new agency;
this was rebuild the machine
- Discipline + inspiration brought back inside
- Marketing = collaboration growth engine
- Siloed thinking replaced by unified execution

Not just an agency move,
a marketing transformation

Launch was clear,
bold & public

Fragmented
ecosystem → unified
operations

From 90 creatives to
9 Operating Units

Shift from fiefdoms
to focus

Shakir Moin
President of Marketing
North America

Custom-built
agency model

One global team:
Creative + media
+ data + strategy

Talent aligned to
business units,
not just brands

NEED FOR UNITY
AND STRUCTURAL FORM

--- **KEY TAKEAWAYS** ---

- Don't fix the agency first, fix the operating model
- Reduce fragmentation by building strategic operating units
- Build a custom agency aligned to your internal org, not above it
- When marketing is embedded inside, it becomes a driver of growth

its brand without diluting it. When Benedetto Vigna took over as CEO, he oversaw structural changes to the company's marketing and commercial organization, aiming to unify the customer experience across digital, retail, and racing. The shift wasn't about chasing volume—it was about aligning storytelling, product strategy, and consumer touchpoints to deepen loyalty and brand prestige. In essence, marketing had to become less of a promotional function and more of a brand stewardship engine.

In both cases, the catalyst for change was the same: Marketing needed to move closer to the business. For P&G, it was about speed and scale. For Ferrari, it was about precision and protection. But the lesson is universal: Restructures are less about fixing marketing and more about elevating it to meet the moment. When done right, they bring marketing back to where it belongs: inside the business, driving growth.

The Ability to Change Is More Important Than Ever

In the past, marketing organizational structures changed gradually—driven by business cycles, leadership changes, or strategic shifts. Today, that pace has accelerated. We're now in a postpandemic era marked by permanent cultural, technological, and operational disruption. In this context, organizational restructuring is no longer a strategic option—it's a necessity.

What's Making Change

First, the COVID-19 pandemic acted as a forcing function for transformation. Remote work became mainstream, prompting companies to reevaluate the geographic footprint of their teams, redefine roles, and reassess agency partnerships. With employees moving out of major urban centers and embracing hybrid work, governance models had to evolve. The classic "all in the same room" marketing meeting is now replaced by asynchronous collaboration tools, necessitating flatter hierarchies and greater clarity in team structure.

Digitization has only intensified this pressure. Consumers now engage with brands across an ever-expanding mix of touchpoints—apps, social media,

Key Structural Trends over the Last Decade

Marketing organizations have undergone profound structural change. What was once a function defined by brand stewardship and campaign execution has transformed into a dynamic, cross-functional growth engine.

	Then	Now
From silos to squads	Teams were typically divided by function—media, creative, PR, digital—all working in linear handoffs.	Many organizations have adopted cross-functional "squads" or "pods" organized around customer journeys, business units, or content streams. These integrated teams blend creative, data, tech, and strategy, working in agile sprints rather than traditional campaigns.
Rise of in-housing	Most creative, media, and digital production was outsourced to agencies.	In-house agencies and content studios are increasingly common, giving marketers greater control, speed, and cost efficiency. Brands like Unilever, P&G, and Adidas have all built internal teams for real-time social, performance media, and content creation.
Marketing as a growth function	Marketing was often seen as a cost center focused on brand and communications.	Marketing is increasingly tied to business outcomes—customer acquisition, lifetime value, and revenue. This has led to closer alignment with sales, product, and finance, often reflected in org charts and reporting lines.
The tech-data-creative convergence	Tech and data lived in separate IT or analytics departments.	Martech, adtech, and data science are embedded into marketing teams. Roles like chief marketing technologies and growth analyst have emerged, and CRM, automation, and AI are core capabilities—not add-ons.
Hybrid, remote, and decentralized teams	Marketing teams were centralized, often colocated at HQ.	With the rise of remote work, teams are distributed across geographies, with flexible governance models and more local empowerment.
Content-led, always-on models	Marketing operated in campaign cycles with set timelines.	Content marketing, social storytelling, and influencer programs demand always-on structures—often supported by editorial calendars and newsroom-style setups.

messaging platforms, and live-streamed content. This omnichannel reality has made legacy marketing models—with their siloed brand teams and linear campaign planning—woefully outdated. Companies must now build agile, data-driven organizations that can activate in real time and iterate based on live insights. "We've brought much of our media strategy in-house on purpose, aiming to ensure our team truly understands media instead of just signing off on proposals," said Eric Lempel, Senior Vice President of Marketing, Sales, Product, and Business Operations at Sony Interactive Entertainment.

Increased competition is another key driver. Challenger brands are more nimble, often born digitally with built-in advantages in customer experience and personalization. Legacy players must restructure not just to survive but to reassert relevance in a crowded marketplace.

But external pressure alone isn't enough. Internally, companies must recognize and embrace the need to restructure—starting with their business models. "An efficient supply chain, an efficient procurement structure, or an efficient distribution organization; these are, I would say, your points of parity. Your real point of differentiation is going to be marketing," says Mukul Deoras, President, Asia-Pacific Division, at Colgate-Palmolive. Brands that rely more heavily on digital commerce, D2C, or subscription-based revenues are more likely to see marketing as a growth engine, not just a cost center. That shift changes how marketing is structured—moving it closer to product, tech, and data teams.

The rise of self-service platforms (like Google Ads, Meta Business Suite, Shopify, etc.) and new martech stacks means marketers can now execute directly. This empowers leaner teams and supports in-housing—where creative, media, or analytics functions are brought back inside the company. But it also demands new skills, new workflows, and new leadership structures. Organizations that restructure to support this—by embedding cross-functional pods or brand squads—can move faster and deliver more relevant, accountable marketing.

AI is also a major disruptor. Whether it's predictive analytics, generative content, or automated media buying, AI is changing how marketing gets done. But AI doesn't just replace jobs—it reshapes them. Companies must restructure to integrate human creativity with machine intelligence, reallocating talent to higher-value, strategic roles while automating the repetitive and routine.

New marketing channels further reinforce the need for change. Social platforms evolve weekly, and the lines between paid, earned, and owned media are increasingly blurred. A rigid, traditional marketing department can't keep up. Instead, organizations are embracing flatter structures, with cross-functional teams empowered to own audience segments, content series, or performance goals across multiple channels.

What's Been the Biggest Change You've Seen in the Last Five Years in Terms of the Way You're Structured, the Way You're Working?

Shakir Moin, President of Marketing, Coca-Cola North America

"The number one problem to solve is, how do we bring brand development consistency across global brands? Number two, how do we become a more efficient machine in the process of doing it? Number three, how do we become more effective?"

Tamara Rogers, Chief Marketing Officer, Haleon

"The biggest changes have of course been media fragmentation, the rise of social and influencers and the ability with digital for the consumer to curate what they experience. In this context, marketers still work to define what the growth opportunity is, who their target audience is, what they do now and what behavior change is required and how best to effect that.

"But now they are trying to think about how they achieve their goals in a significantly more complex ecosystem. How to build in the consumer's mind a memory structure of the brand, an association that can be activated to drive conversion when the moment to buy arises. And how to do that with efficiency and effectiveness.

"At Haleon, we've been trying to create brand growth strategies and plans that help provide direction on where to play and how to win but also provoke our marketers to apply their powers of critical thinking and problem-solving skills to greater effect."

Mukul Deoras, President, Asia-Pacific Division, Colgate-Palmolive

"There is huge fragmentation happening in marketing across tools, activities, and even the processes that we have. As it becomes more fragmented, and therefore distracting, the more we need to be focused on the brand and maintain integrity."

Cheryl Guerin, Executive Vice President of Global Brand Strategy and Innovation, Mastercard

"The pace of change is unbelievably fast, and so much of what we do today is tied to digital/technology platforms or unique experiences. In addition, with so much media fragmentation the fight for attention has never been greater. We are exposed to over 5,000 messages a day and only a few will stick.

"We have pivoted away from traditional advertising that disrupts the experience, and we are focused on enabling meaningful and engaging experiences. This requires rich insights, constant innovation, and infrastructure that enables agile and real-time marketing.

"It used to be a particular group who was savvy in new tech and drivers of innovation. To stay ahead of the competition, you need every group innovating, every group understanding how to leverage technology, but you also need SMEs that can quickly advance commercialization."

Colin Westcott-Pitt, Global Chief Brand Officer, Glanbia

"Retail media has added another level of opportunity and complexity for brands. It has highlighted the need for an integrated approach between marketing and sales or risk investments that may overlap and diminish return."

Mike Tripp, Group Vice President of Marketing, Toyota Motor NA

"The skills and mindsets that are important today that just weren't as critical even five years ago. For example, the understanding of data and analytics and the impact of technology across the board. I don't think most clients have quite figured out the balance between outsourcing and in-housing those skills."

Edward Bell, General Manager, Brand, Insights and Marketing Communications, Cathay Pacific

"We've invested a lot more in data-driven marketing, in terms of the utilization of first-party data and propensity modeling in the way that we talk to our members. We've made great strides in terms of conversion media."

The Path Forward: From Reactive to Proactive

Ultimately, organizational restructuring isn't about reacting to crises—it's about preparing for continuous change. "Good or bad marketing will show its impact not today but three or five years from now," says Colgate-Palmolive's Mukul Deoras. The companies that thrive will be those that treat structure not as a fixed design but as a living, adaptive system. They'll align their marketing teams with how their customers behave, not with outdated job titles. They'll invest in platforms, training, and leadership that turn data into action and culture into competitive advantage.

Marketing is no longer a department. It's a system of capabilities, technology, content, and people—working in sync to drive growth. Restructuring is the first step to making that system work better, from the inside out.

Reinventing a Legacy Through Marketing Transformation

By the late 2010s, Mattel—a storied toy company behind brands like Barbie, Hot Wheels, and Fisher-Price—found itself at a crossroads. Faced with digital-native competitors, declining toy sales, and changing consumer expectations, its relevance was slipping. The world had moved on, but Mattel hadn't. That changed under CEO Ynon Kreiz, who recognized that Mattel needed to stop marketing toys and start marketing stories.

The company's transformation was both strategic and structural. Kreiz reframed Mattel as an IP-driven entertainment company, not just a toy manufacturer. This demanded a complete reimagining of the marketing organization. No longer could campaigns be built around product launches alone—they had to live across film, streaming, retail, gaming, and social platforms. This shift required Mattel's marketers to move from siloed brand teams to integrated content and storytelling units.

Marketing leadership brought in top talent from the worlds of media and entertainment, including Richard Dickson and Lisa McKnight, who helped reposition Barbie from a dated stereotype to a modern, empowering icon. The film *Barbie* became a cultural event—not a commercial. That didn't just happen; it was the result of embedding brand narrative and cultural relevance into the heart of Mattel's marketing structure.

The timing was pitch perfect. Post pandemic, families sought connection, nostalgia, and shared experiences. Mattel's new model was built to meet those needs—leaning into digital, embracing influencers, and building long-term content pipelines instead of short-term promotions.

The result? Mattel didn't just become cool again—it became culturally indispensable. The marketing organization transformed from a cost center to a strategic growth engine, capable of building multiplatform franchises. In the process, Mattel proved that even the most traditional companies can evolve—if they're willing to open up their brand, structure, and story to the future.

How Do You Know Your Organization Is Ready for Change?

One of the toughest calls a marketer has to make isn't about which campaign to run or what media to buy—it's knowing when the organization itself needs to change.

"If the strategy is changing, your structure evolves too," says Coca-Cola's Shakir Moin. "As we evolve towards a network way of marketing, we have redesigned our marketing organization for global consistency, which is facilitated by more direct and clear connections with various teams across markets. It also leads to faster talent redeployment and enables us to cut waste. As an example, in North America, we are down from 400 tactical initiatives to eight big initiatives that take up 80% of our resources."

Unlike a declining sales graph or a busted creative brief, organizational inertia isn't always obvious. But for marketers paying attention, the signals are there. And when they start piling up, it's not just a sign—it's a siren.

What Are the Signals?

- **Speed mismatch:** If it takes your team twelve weeks to launch something your competitor turned around in two, you have a structural problem. Decision-making bottlenecks, endless internal reviews, and siloed functions are symptoms of an outdated operating model—not just a time management issue.

- **Fragmented consumer experience:** If your brand looks and sounds different across every touchpoint—social, retail, email, app—it's a sign your marketing organization is working in disconnected streams. A modern consumer expects a unified experience, and that requires a unified team structure.

- **Underutilized tech stack:** You've invested in data platforms, CRM systems, AI tools—but your team is still planning campaigns using PowerPoint decks and Excel spreadsheets. If the tools are there but the transformation isn't, your people and processes need reworking.

- **Rising costs, flat outcomes:** You're spending more with less impact. This could be a media issue—or it could be that your organization isn't structured to maximize value. Complexity often eats ROI.

- **Talent turnover:** If your best marketers are leaving for more agile, innovative organizations, take the hint. Structure is strategy, and people want to work where they can move quickly and make an impact.

Does This Require a Full Organizational Restructure?

Not necessarily. Sometimes, change can happen within marketing alone—without waiting for a global reorg. It can begin with one brand team piloting a new model, a cross-functional squad built around a consumer segment, or a tighter integration between media, creative, and data roles. Agile marketing pods or "centers of excellence" can exist within the old structure while proving the case for broader change.

Change doesn't have to be announced with a fanfare and a two-hundred-slide deck. It can begin in the margins—one team, one product, one campaign—and grow outward as results prove the model.

Can It Happen Without Changing the Agency Model?

In some cases, yes—but it's unlikely to be sustainable. Your internal structure and external partners need to mirror each other. If you're organizing around real-time content and consumer moments but your agency is still working in quarterly campaign cycles, you're setting yourself up for friction. The best agency relationships today are adaptive, embedded, and built around outcomes—not outputs. This means that at some point, a structural shift inside marketing often triggers a corresponding change in agency engagement.

Can It Happen Without Stakeholder Buy-In?

Technically, yes. But strategically? Not for long. The best marketing transformations don't happen in isolation. You need IT to support your tech integration. You need finance to align on investment and ROI. You need HR to hire different kinds of talent. If marketing is changing but the rest of the business isn't listening, your transformation will stall. Early buy-in from the right stakeholders—especially the C-suite—is a multiplier.

"Our leadership team has a strong consumer pedigree," says Tamara Rogers of Haleon. "Both our CEO and CFO for example have an FMCG background and appreciate brands, see them as true assets on our balance sheet, the importance of marketing and the importance of innovation. I find myself often engaging with them on how well we are building superior brands, how our share of market is progressing, how well are we competing and of course how well we use our A&P to build and strengthen our brands and drive conversion to purchase."

How Do You Know You're Ready?

You know you're ready when *not* changing feels riskier than evolving. You feel the gap between what your consumers want and what your team can deliver. You see the future coming and realize your current organization can't get you there. When that moment arrives, don't wait for permission. Pilot, prove, and show. Transformation doesn't start with a big idea—it starts with a brave marketer willing to lead from inside.

What to Consider Before Making Change

Transforming a marketing organization is like rewiring a jet midflight. The stakes are high, the timing is critical, and the risks can derail even the best intentions. So before jumping into change, marketers need to pause, breathe, and plan with precision. The truth is, successful marketing transformation isn't just about ambition—it's about alignment, agility, and execution.

1. **Clarify the "Why"**

   Before launching into transformation, marketers must first answer the most important question: "Why are we doing this?" Is it because customer expectations have evolved? Because the current model is too slow, too expensive, or too fragmented? Because the business is shifting from product led to experience led? Without a clear "why," the initiative risks becoming a costly vanity project rather than a strategic engine for growth.

   Transformation must solve a business problem. Whether it's aligning to new revenue streams, expanding into new channels, or rethinking the customer journey, the purpose has to be crystal clear—and tied to measurable outcomes.

2. **Audit Your Current State**

   You can't get to where you're going if you don't understand where you are. That means taking a hard look at your current structure, skills, systems, and spend. What functions are duplicative? Where are the silos? Are your teams operating in real time or still stuck in waterfall planning?

   Benchmark your internal performance, agency partnerships, and use of technology. Don't be afraid to call out the inefficiencies. This is the diagnosis phase—and honesty is nonnegotiable.

3. **Secure Leadership Alignment**

   Transformation isn't just a marketing project—it's a business decision. Get buy-in early from key stakeholders: the CEO, CFO, CIO, CHRO. You'll need support on budget, systems, hiring, and potentially cultural shifts. Marketing may lead the charge, but success depends on shared ownership across functions.

One smart tactic? Tie your marketing transformation goals to the broader business strategy. If the company is prioritizing growth in D2C, your reorg can focus on digital acceleration. If cost efficiency is the mandate, show how a leaner, tech-powered marketing model delivers more with less.

4. **Design Around the Consumer**

Resist the urge to organize around job titles or internal departments. Instead, structure your teams around the consumer journey. Build squads or pods responsible for key touchpoints—acquisition, retention, experience, loyalty. Bring together creative, data, media, and product folks in the same team.

Today's most effective marketing organizations are cross-functional and outcome driven. They're built for speed, learning, and iteration—not hierarchy.

5. **Plan for Talent and Tools**

Marketing transformation often reveals a skills gap. You might need fewer brand managers and more marketing technologists, analysts, and content creators. Consider your hiring road map early—and don't forget upskilling your existing talent.

Likewise, assess your tech stack. The best structure in the world will fail if your tools can't support it. Invest in platforms that connect data, automate workflow, and empower creativity.

6. **Pilot First; Scale Fast**

Best practice says, "Don't boil the ocean." Start with a pilot—one brand, one market, or one business unit. Test the new model, track the outcomes, and refine the approach. Once you've proven success, scale it with momentum and confidence. This approach reduces risk, builds internal champions, and creates a blueprint for broader adoption.

7. **Communicate Relentlessly**

   Change is hard. It brings fear, confusion, and resistance. That's why communication is your secret weapon. Share the vision, explain the process, and show the wins—early and often. Involve your teams in shaping the journey. Transparency builds trust, and trust fuels transformation.

8. **Measure What Matters**

   Transformation isn't complete when the org chart changes—it's complete when performance improves. Set clear key performance indicators (KPIs): campaign velocity, ROI, brand engagement, customer satisfaction. Track them religiously. What gets measured gets managed—and what gets managed gets better.

Disney: A Tale of Marketing Restructure and Strategic Realignment

In 2020, the Walt Disney Company undertook one of its most significant organizational restructures in decades, with marketing at the heart of the transformation. The trigger? A rapidly shifting entertainment landscape, accelerated by the pandemic, where streaming became the new front line of consumer engagement. Disney responded by reorganizing around content distribution rather than content creation—a bold pivot for a legacy brand steeped in storytelling.

Disney created a centralized division: Media and Entertainment Distribution (DMED), designed to control all distribution, advertising, and even marketing functions. The goal was to streamline operations and prioritize platforms like Disney+, Hulu, and ESPN+. Marketing that once sat close to creative teams was now part of a distribution powerhouse focused on data and digital scale.

Initially, the move made sense. It promised integration, efficiency, and a performance-led approach to content promotion. But cracks emerged. Creatives and marketers voiced concerns that centralizing marketing decisions separated them from the heart of the content. The magic of Disney's brand—built on emotional storytelling—risked being overshadowed by algorithm-driven messaging.

Recently, under new CEO Bob Iger's return, Disney reversed parts of this restructure. Marketing functions were gradually realigned closer to content divisions like Disney Studios, Marvel, and Pixar. The lesson? While scale and efficiency matter, creativity, cultural resonance, and proximity to content creation remain nonnegotiable for brand-led organizations.

Key takeaways:
- Restructures must balance efficiency with brand intimacy.
- Centralization works best when it enhances—not dilutes—creative storytelling.
- Organizational design should support the company's core value proposition. For Disney, that's emotion and imagination, not just distribution metrics.

Disney's experience shows that even the most admired brands must continuously tune their structure to serve both business goals and brand essence—without losing the magic.

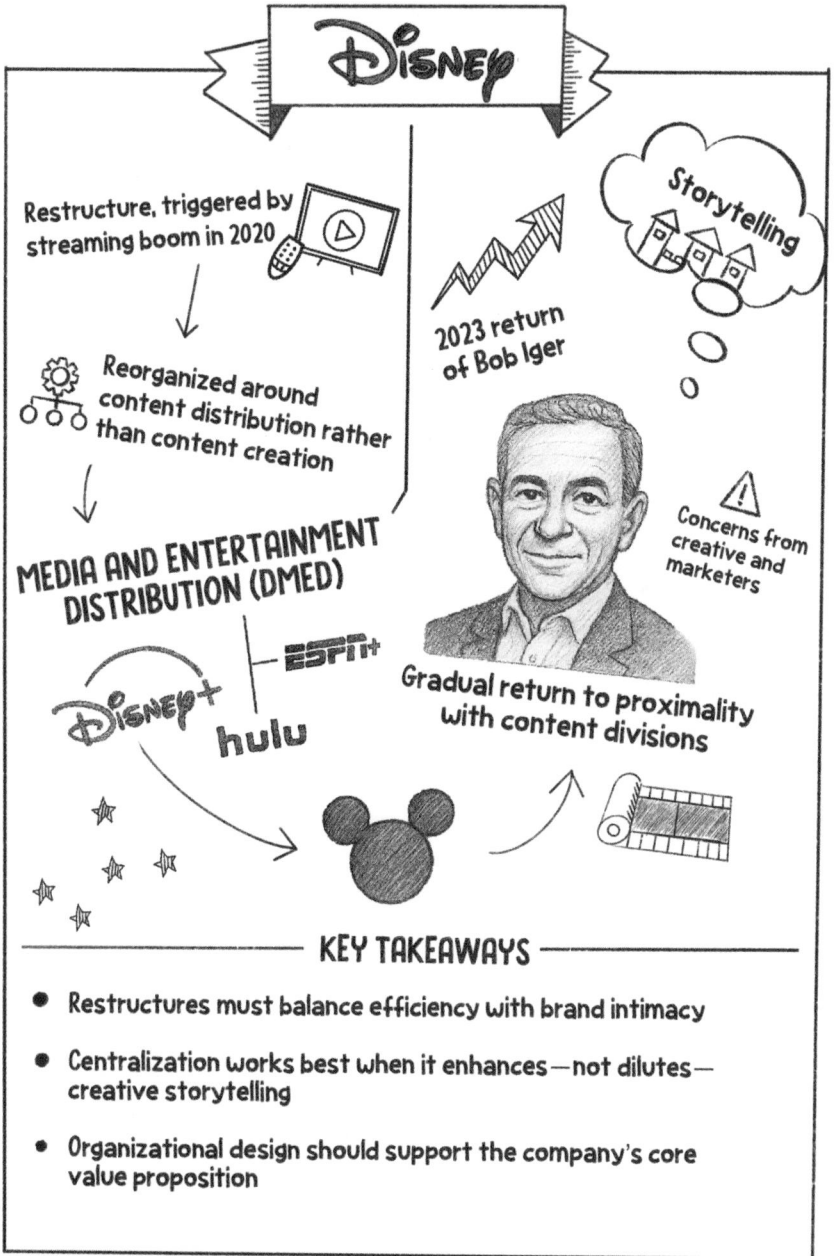

DISNEP

Restructure, triggered by streaming boom in 2020

Reorganized around content distribution rather than content creation

MEDIA AND ENTERTAINMENT DISTRIBUTION (DMED)

ESPN+

DISNEP+

hulu

2023 return of Bob Iger

Storytelling

Concerns from creative and marketers

Gradual return to proximality with content divisions

KEY TAKEAWAYS

- Restructures must balance efficiency with brand intimacy

- Centralization works best when it enhances — not dilutes — creative storytelling

- Organizational design should support the company's core value proposition

Netflix: Marketing Reinvention in a Streaming World

As the pioneer of the streaming revolution, Netflix built its empire on product innovation and data-driven content. But by the late 2010s, its marketing organization was lagging behind its growth. The company's rapid global expansion, combined with increasing competition from Disney+, Amazon, and local players, exposed a fragmented and reactive marketing model. Campaigns were often siloed by region, lacked cohesion, and failed to fully leverage Netflix's vast cultural capital.

In response, Netflix embarked on a marketing transformation. The company centralized its marketing structure to ensure a more unified global voice while still enabling local relevance. It aligned teams around content categories (e.g., film, series, unscripted) rather than geography, enabling closer collaboration between marketers and the creative pipeline.

Netflix also shifted from purely performance-driven campaigns to emotional, culture-first storytelling. A standout example was the global marketing effort behind *Stranger Things*, season four, which blended traditional media, experiential activations, and social storytelling to reignite fan fervor. Marketing became a strategic extension of the content itself, not just an add-on.

Critically, Netflix also invested in building its in-house creative capabilities, giving teams more agility and control. As a result, the brand could respond faster to cultural moments, tailor content promotion by audience behavior, and own the narrative in real time.

Key takeaways:

- Align marketing with content creation—not just distribution—to amplify cultural impact.
- Centralization works best when it enhances speed, consistency, and collaboration across markets.
- Emotional storytelling and community building should be central pillars, even for data-driven brands.
- In-house capabilities can increase agility—but they require investment in talent and tools.

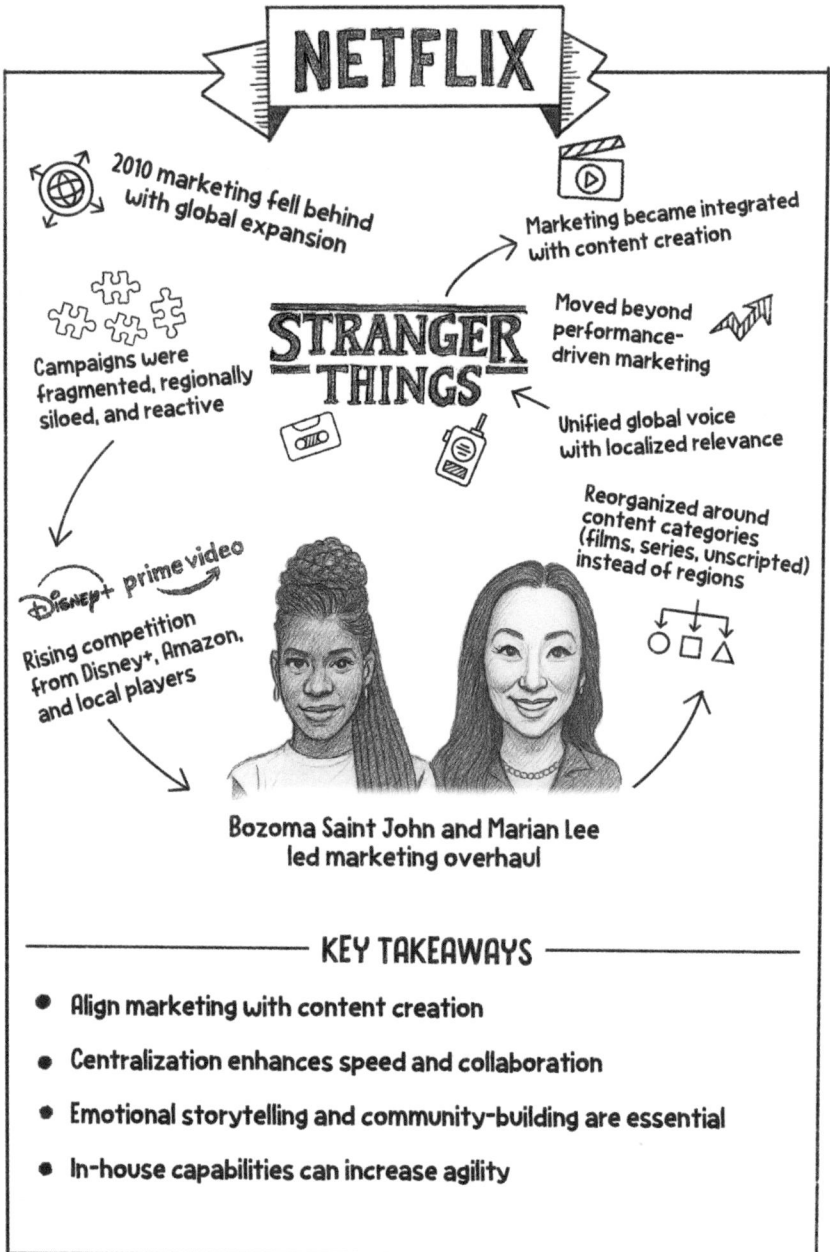

NETFLIX

2010 marketing fell behind with global expansion

Marketing became integrated with content creation

Campaigns were fragmented, regionally siloed, and reactive

STRANGER THINGS

Moved beyond performance-driven marketing

Unified global voice with localized relevance

Reorganized around content categories (films, series, unscripted) instead of regions

Rising competition from Disney+, Amazon, and local players

Disney+ prime video

Bozoma Saint John and Marian Lee led marketing overhaul

— KEY TAKEAWAYS —

- Align marketing with content creation
- Centralization enhances speed and collaboration
- Emotional storytelling and community-building are essential
- In-house capabilities can increase agility

Chapter 2
How Marketing Decisions
Get Made

When we started advising marketers, we kept bumping into a peculiar problem. Everyone wanted great marketing—but nobody could agree on how it should actually run. Was it the strategy? The people? The tech? The process? The structure? Yes.

The truth is, most companies are flying the marketing plane while still building the cockpit. And that cockpit—how marketing is organized, resourced, and activated—is what we call the marketing operating model. It sounds dry. But it's anything but.

At its best, a marketing operating model is your secret weapon. It sets the rhythm for how you plan campaigns, build teams, run media, launch brands, and (hopefully) create goosebumps. It includes the strategy, yes—but also the talent, the tools, the processes, the governance. All the stuff that rarely wins Cannes Lions but wins the business.

And like any system, the structure matters.

Do you centralize for consistency? Decentralize for speed? Do you try to do both and call it "hybrid" while quietly pulling your hair out? We've seen global marketers who run like the Swiss railway system—like clockwork and aligned. We've also seen the Wild West, where every market is doing its own thing with its own playbook and hoping the brand shows up somewhere in the mix.

Neither model is inherently better. A centralized approach works wonders for control, scale, and efficiency—especially in regulated industries or when brand integrity is nonnegotiable. A decentralized model makes sense when you need agility, cultural nuance, or fast responses to local dynamics. And the hybrid? Well, that's where most brands end up. It's the art of balance. And like all art—it takes work.

But this isn't about models for models' sake. It's about making marketing count. Inside.

"You have to organize your company in such a way that you have the appropriate structure from a management standpoint," says Mike Tripp, Toyota North America's Group Vice President of Marketing. "How many people can you manage and lead? Having a culture that is more agile, where you aren't beholden to traditional reporting structures, is critical because there will be times where you need speed in decision-making and have to throw it out. You have to make sure the structure and culture support working in a more agile, nimble way."

That means giving marketers the structure to succeed, the space to lead, and the skills to deliver. It means replacing chaos with clarity, silos with synergy, and PowerPoint with performance. Because when the operating model is right, the marketing starts to sing.

How Have You Managed the Complexity of Global and Local Teams, Especially in a Category as Complex and Market Sensitive as Healthcare?

Tamara Rogers, Chief Marketing Officer, Haleon

"Working in an international company you face the complexity of a global/ local matrix—the complexity comes when there is a lack of clarity around who does what, and the potential is unlocked when you have the right people working through challenges together. Over the years I've resourced more heavily global teams, then shifting to more local. Having people move between the two is critical—building an appreciation of what a role takes, what is needed and why, makes a huge difference.

"Healthcare is different to other CPG sectors with more local regulatory environments, so getting the balance of resourcing, the right capability in the right places is key. This is particularly true for innovation—in some countries the Board of Health locally needs to approve your claims and your advertising content. I think it's important that whatever seat you are in—in a global role or a local role—you are one team on any particular brand. What I love is when I can walk into a room and not know who is global and who is local!

"Whilst media is fragmenting and sources of trust are shifting, I still believe in the power of creative and of ideas. We take an approach of Hero and Halo content. Hero is the core of the idea expressed in assets that multiple markets require, usually generated globally, ready for adaptation, transcreation, etc. Halo is generated locally, inspired by the core idea but intended to amplify appropriately for the country. Sometimes this content can also travel. Some is uniquely local—much for example of what we create in China, is China for China. It's all stored and tagged in our DAM—to try and avoid waste—check the DAM and only originate if necessary."

Decoding Centralization: Pulling the Strings Tighter

A few years ago, the word *centralization* would've made most marketers shift uncomfortably in their seats. It sounded bureaucratic. The kind of thing you did when you wanted to kill creativity and slow everything down. Not anymore.

A recent Gartner survey found that 65 percent of marketing organizations were already "fully" or "partially" centralized. This marks a notable progression from two years prior, which reported that 66 percent were transitioning toward centralization. Recently, nearly half of marketing organizations reported undergoing restructuring in the prior year—highlighting that structure is still in flux.

In a world defined by uncertainty—pandemics, supply chain chaos, media fragmentation—marketers realized something: Centralization isn't about control. It's about stability. It's the ability to move fast because you're aligned. To act boldly because your foundation is solid.

Here's what centralized marketing actually looks like on the inside:

- Decisions come from the top—and they come fast.
- Processes are standardized. Everyone knows the playbook.
- Local teams take the brief, not the lead.
- Budgets, data, and brand get handled by the people with the clearest line of sight.

Sound rigid? Maybe. But it's also efficient.
Done well, here's what centralization means:

- Fewer meetings. Faster rollouts.
- One brand voice, not fifteen accents.
- Budgets that stretch further because they're managed as one.
- Analytics that aren't lost in translation across regions.

Brand, strategy, budgeting, analytics—these are the areas where centralization wins. But let's be clear. It's not perfect. If you centralize everything, you risk killing local innovation. Morale can drop. Decision-making can bottleneck. Some of the best ideas get stuck in the wrong inbox. And when the world changes? You might move too slowly to keep up. The trick isn't choosing centralization. It's knowing what to centralize—and what to let go. Because the best marketing operating models don't just run—they adapt.

Shifting Toward a Centralized Marketing Organization

A shift to centralized marketing is a significant transformation, but when executed with clear strategy, collaboration, and the right tools, it can drive efficiency, stronger brand equity, and improved marketing performance. Ensuring regional flexibility within a centralized framework is key to long-term success.

1. Establish a clear vision and business case:

- Define why centralization is needed (e.g., cost savings, brand consistency, efficiency).
- Communicate how the new structure will support the business goal.
- Get executive leadership buy-in to drive the change effectively.

2. Conduct an audit of current marketing operations:

Assess the existing decentralized setup:

- Identify redundancies, inefficiencies, and inconsistencies.
- Understand local market needs and challenges.
- Gather feedback from regional marketing teams, sales, and key stakeholders.

3. Define the centralized model:

Decide on the level of centralization:

- Fully centralized: All marketing decisions and execution are handled by a central team.

- Hybrid: Strategy, branding, and major campaigns are centralized, but some execution is localized.

Clearly define roles, responsibilities, and decision-making authority.

4. Build the right team and skill sets:

- Assess existing talent and fill skill gaps with new hires or training.
- Define leadership roles to manage global and local marketing needs.
- Foster a collaborative culture where regional teams feel valued.

5. Standardize processes and workflows:

- Develop SOPs (standard operating procedures) for campaign execution, approvals, and reporting.
- Implement project management tools to streamline operations.
- Define clear escalation points and feedback loops.

6. Invest in the right technology:

Implement a centralized martech stack for the following:

- Content management (e.g., DAM—digital asset management).
- Marketing automation and CRM.
- Data analytics and performance tracking.
- Ensure all teams have access to the right tools and training.

7. Establish a unified brand strategy:

- Create a global brand playbook covering messaging, tone, visual identity, and guidelines.
- Ensure regional teams have access to preapproved templates and assets.
- Regularly review and update guidelines based on feedback.

8. Implement a strong change management plan:

- Communicate early and often to ensure buy-in from regional teams.
- Address concerns around autonomy, flexibility, and decision-making.
- Highlight quick wins to show the benefits of centralization.
- Provide ongoing training to support the transition.

9. Foster collaboration between central and local teams:

- Set up regular check-ins between global and regional teams.
- Encourage a feedback-driven culture to refine the approach.
- Create internal communities (e.g., shared Slack channels, knowledge hubs) to share insights and best practices.

10. Measure success and iterate:

- Define key KPIs to track success (e.g., cost savings, campaign effectiveness, lead generation, brand consistency).
- Use data-driven insights to refine strategies and improve operations.
- Be flexible—adjust processes based on team feedback and market demands.

Airbnb: Global Brand, Local Soul

As a global hospitality platform operating in over 220 countries and regions, Airbnb has always had an ambitious mission: to help anyone belong anywhere. But as it scaled rapidly, it ran into a problem familiar to many global marketers: How do you build one brand that still feels personal everywhere?

By the late 2010s, Airbnb's marketing was showing signs of strain. Regional teams operated with high autonomy, often creating campaigns independently. This led to fragmented messaging, uneven quality, and missed opportunities to leverage shared insights or scale efficiencies. The brand's voice—once iconic—was starting to get lost in the noise.

To address this, Airbnb centralized its marketing function. A new global marketing team (GMT) was built at its San Francisco HQ, charged with setting global brand strategy, messaging, and creative direction. Regional teams remained, but their role shifted to local execution—ensuring cultural nuance while staying on brand.

The GMT introduced a unified creative and analytics platform, allowing teams to collaborate in real time and share performance data globally. Campaigns like "Made Possible by Hosts" exemplified this new model: born from a global insight, shaped by regional storytelling, and executed with consistency across touchpoints.

The results were immediate. Brand consistency improved. Media efficiency rose through centralized planning and buying. And campaigns became more scalable—with creative tailored, not reinvented, for local markets.

Airbnb's centralized model didn't dilute local voice—it amplified it within a coherent global system.

Key takeaways:

- Centralization can unlock brand consistency and operational efficiency without sacrificing local relevance.
- A global creative core paired with regional adaptation creates scale and nuance.
- Unified data and collaboration tools are critical enablers of agile, market-informed campaigns.
- Centralized marketing works best when it empowers—not replaces—local execution.

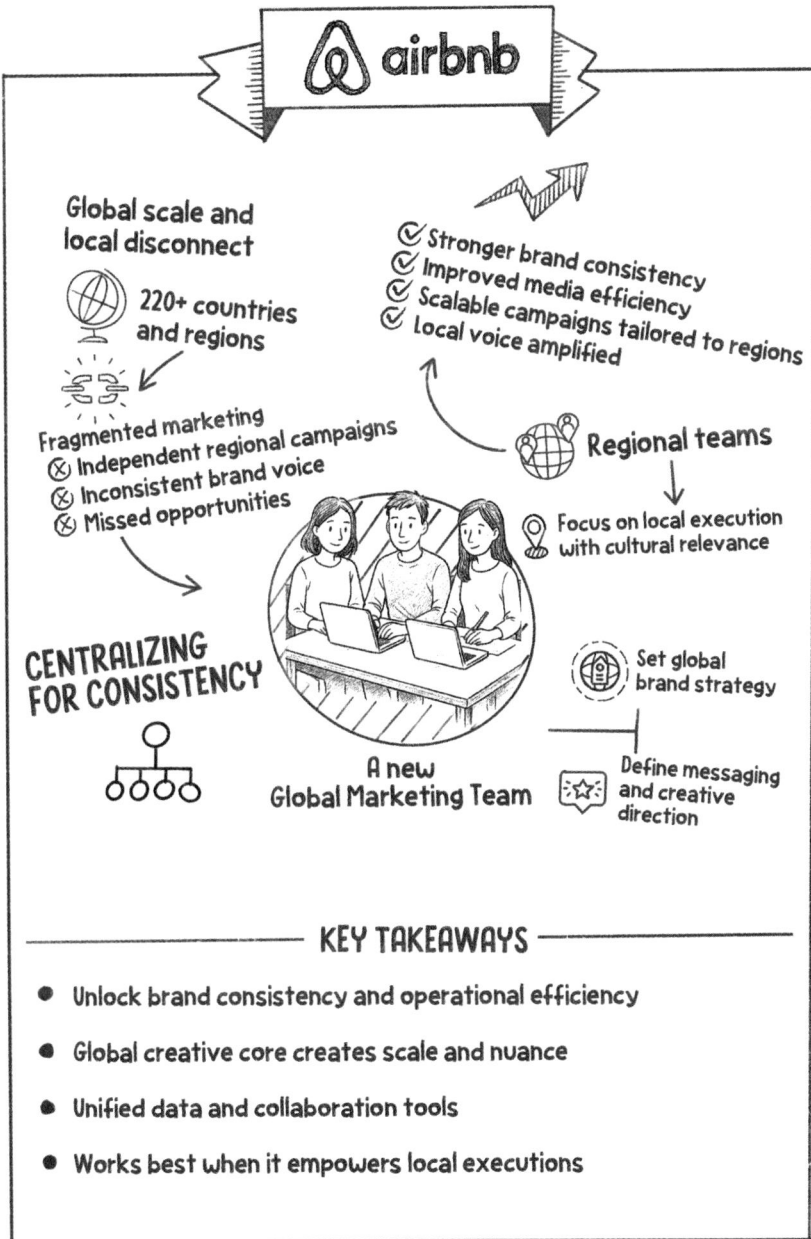

airbnb

Global scale and local disconnect

220+ countries and regions

Fragmented marketing
- ⊗ Independent regional campaigns
- ⊗ Inconsistent brand voice
- ⊗ Missed opportunities

✓ Stronger brand consistency
✓ Improved media efficiency
✓ Scalable campaigns tailored to regions
✓ Local voice amplified

Regional teams

Focus on local execution with cultural relevance

CENTRALIZING FOR CONSISTENCY

A new Global Marketing Team

Set global brand strategy

Define messaging and creative direction

KEY TAKEAWAYS

- Unlock brand consistency and operational efficiency
- Global creative core creates scale and nuance
- Unified data and collaboration tools
- Works best when it empowers local executions

Decoding Decentralization: Letting Go to Move Faster

At some point, every marketing leader faces the same question: "Should we hold the reins tighter—or loosen the grip?" For many global brands, the answer lately has been clear: Decentralize. Why? Because markets don't wait for HQ. And customers don't care if your brand guidelines are still "in review."

A decentralized marketing structure flips the script. Instead of decisions crawling their way up the org chart, they're made at the edges—by people closest to the market, the customer, and the opportunity. Think less pyramid, more web. Authority isn't hoarded. It's handed out, with trust.

"The more that you can organize yourselves around expertise as opposed to geographical starting points, the better, more interesting, more effective you'll be at business," says Glanbia's Global Chief Brand Officer Colin West-cott-Pitt. "You could be a consumer expert, you could be a digital expert, you could be a media channel expert. That's more fruitful and helpful than saying it's global or local."

In the best decentralized systems, decision-making sits where the action is. Teams on the ground are empowered—not just to execute but to experiment. Local marketers don't need permission to try something bold. They own the results. And the learning.

What does that look like in practice?

- Social teams adapting content in real time to match local trends
- PR leads building relationships with regional media on their terms
- Field marketers launching events without waiting for a global "go"
- Cross-functional teams solving problems without fifteen approvals

The upside is real: speed, relevance, morale, and often breakthrough ideas. Decentralized models have been behind some of the most culturally resonant marketing moves in recent years—because the people are making them live the culture they're marketing into.

But let's be honest. It's not all upside. Decentralization can create a mess. Without alignment, brands drift. Without coordination, you risk duplicate work, inconsistent messages, and missed efficiencies. Strategy can fray if there's no central thread pulling things together. That's why the best decentralized systems don't abandon structure. They redefine it. Governance doesn't disappear—it becomes a framework, not a bottleneck. Global defines the "what" and "why." Local decides the "how." Because when you get it right, decentralization doesn't mean chaos. It means creativity. Responsiveness. Ownership.

Shifting to a Decentralized Marketing Organization

A successful decentralized marketing organization strikes the right balance between autonomy and alignment. While local teams drive execution, a strong strategic framework, standardized processes, and collaboration tools ensure the brand remains cohesive. Companies that invest in communication, data-driven insights, and agility will see the best results from a decentralized approach.

1. Clear strategic alignment across teams

- While execution is decentralized, there must be a clear company-wide marketing vision and objectives.
- Central leadership should set strategic guidelines to ensure alignment across markets.
- A shared framework helps maintain consistency while allowing for localized flexibility.

2. Strong local autonomy and ownership

- Local marketing teams should have the authority to make decisions quickly and independently.
- Teams must be empowered to respond to market-specific trends, customer behaviors, and cultural nuances.
- Autonomy leads to faster innovation and responsiveness.

3. Consistent brand governance and guidelines

- Even with decentralized execution, a unified brand identity is crucial.
- A well-documented brand playbook should provide clear guidelines on the following:
  - Brand messaging
  - Visual identity
  - Tone of voice
  - Approved marketing assets
- Centralized oversight ensures the brand remains recognizable across markets.

4. Strong internal communication and collaboration

- A successful decentralized model fosters open communication between global and local teams.
- Regular knowledge-sharing should be done through the following:
  - Internal wikis or shared knowledge hubs
  - Cross-functional marketing meetings
  - Regional success stories and case studies
- Collaboration tools like Slack, Microsoft Teams, or Asana help keep teams connected.

5. Data-driven decision-making

- While execution is decentralized, data collection should be standardized and centralized for better insights.
- All teams should have access to the following:
  - Customer insights
  - Performance analytics
  - Market trends

- A centralized analytics team can provide data-backed recommendations to local teams.

6. The right balance of technology and tools

- Shared martech infrastructure ensures seamless operations, even with decentralized teams.
- Key tools include the following:
  - Marketing automation platforms (HubSpot, Marketo)
  - Content management systems (CMS) for localized content adaptation
  - CRM systems (Salesforce, Zoho) to ensure unified customer data
  - Collaboration software for easy asset sharing

7. Agile and flexible operations

- Decentralized marketing thrives when teams can pivot quickly based on local trends.
- Agile methodologies (such as scrum-based marketing) help teams iterate and improve campaigns based on real-time feedback.
- Encouraging experimentation and innovation leads to more effective localized campaigns.

8. Scalable budgeting and resource allocation

- Budgets should be flexible enough to allow local teams to allocate resources where needed.
- A balance between central funding for major initiatives and local control over daily spending works best.
- Performance-based budget adjustments ensure high-impact campaigns get more investment.

9. Strong leadership and local accountability

- Local teams should have clear ownership of results.
- Each region or business unit should have marketing leaders responsible for driving performance.
- Regular check-ins with central leadership ensure accountability without excessive oversight.

10. Continuous learning and development

- Decentralized teams should be equipped with the latest marketing knowledge and tools.
- Ongoing training should be provided in the following:
  - Digital marketing trends
  - Analytics and data interpretation
  - Brand compliance and storytelling
- Internal training programs, workshops, and mentorship opportunities help upskill teams.

Nestlé: Local First, Global Always

With over two thousand brands and operations in 180-plus countries, Nestlé isn't just a global business—it's a local one, everywhere. But that scale comes with a challenge: How do you build a unified brand while staying culturally relevant from Lagos to Lima to Tokyo?

By the mid-2010s, Nestlé knew a top-down marketing model wouldn't cut it. Local preferences were too specific. Consumer behavior was shifting fast. And central command was slowing things down.

The company leaned into decentralization—not as a workaround but as a strategic advantage. Local markets were empowered to lead marketing execution, grounded in consumer insight and cultural understanding. The global team stepped back from control and stepped into enablement: setting broad guardrails, sharing data, and investing in shared tools.

Campaigns became hyperrelevant. In India, Maggi positioned itself as a five-minute fix for working parents. In Japan, Nescafé tapped into the slow coffee movement, launching boutique cafés and premium blends. No central team could've dreamed those up. Global teams still mattered—just differently. They provided creative frameworks, tech infrastructure, and access to best practices across regions. More importantly, they learned when to listen instead of lead. This wasn't decentralization as an escape hatch. It was decentralization as a deliberate operating model.

Key takeaways:

- Empowering local teams with execution authority drives relevance and responsiveness in diverse markets.
- Global should act as an enabler, not a gatekeeper—providing tools, standards, and shared learning.
- Strong cultural insight and autonomy fuel innovation and faster decision-making.
- A clear framework from HQ helps prevent brand drift without stifling creativity. True global marketing leadership comes from balancing consistency with context.

Nestlé's approach proves that decentralization isn't about losing control—it's about gaining traction where it matters most: with the consumer.

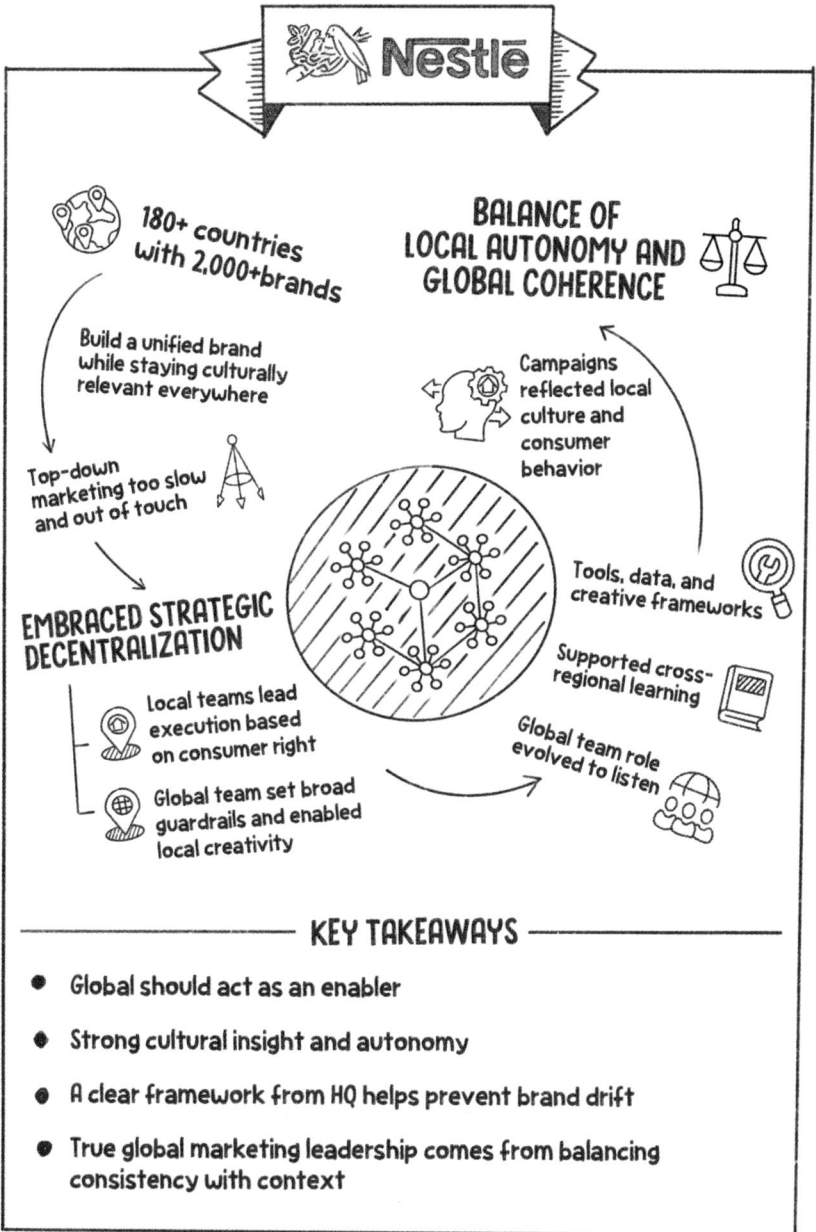

Nestlē

180+ countries with 2,000+ brands

BALANCE OF LOCAL AUTONOMY AND GLOBAL COHERENCE

Build a unified brand while staying culturally relevant everywhere

Campaigns reflected local culture and consumer behavior

Top-down marketing too slow and out of touch

Tools, data, and creative frameworks

EMBRACED STRATEGIC DECENTRALIZATION

Supported cross-regional learning

- Local teams lead execution based on consumer right

- Global team set broad guardrails and enabled local creativity

Global team role evolved to listen

KEY TAKEAWAYS

- Global should act as an enabler

- Strong cultural insight and autonomy

- A clear framework from HQ helps prevent brand drift

- True global marketing leadership comes from balancing consistency with context

Rethinking Hybrid: The Hub-and-Spoke Model That Actually Works

Somewhere between the rigidity of centralization and the chaos of decentralization sits a middle path that global marketers are increasingly leaning into: the hub-and-spoke model. At first glance, it sounds like corporate jargon. But dig deeper, and you find that it's actually one of the few structures that lets marketing scale and stay smart.

Imagine a wheel. The hub is your central marketing team—where the strategy lives, where the budget is set, where the brand voice is defined. The spokes are your markets, regions, or business units—each with boots on the ground, tasked with bringing that strategy to life in context. The model works when both parts know their role, trust each other, and talk regularly. It's not new. But it's newly urgent.

In today's world, marketers need to move fast, stay on brand, and speak local fluently. That's the tension the hub-and-spoke model resolves—if it's done right.

Here's why it works:

- Efficiency without sameness: The hub standardizes what matters—like brand guidelines, campaign assets, and tech infrastructure—so local teams don't have to start from scratch.
- Scale without losing soul: Local spokes retain the freedom to tailor, translate, and sometimes toss what doesn't work.
- Smarts shared both ways: The best ideas can come from anywhere, and the model allows for fast cross-pollination across markets.
  But let's be honest—it's not easy:

- Too much hub? You stifle local creativity.
- Too little? You lose control, and your brand becomes a global whisper.
- Communication gaps? That's where the model breaks down. Fast.

This structure demands real-time collaboration, mutual respect, and a shared appetite for clarity. Without that, you're left with a process map nobody follows.

Here's where hub-and-spoke marketing shines:

- **Brand governance:** The hub protects the brand. The spokes adapt it. Think of global retailers that keep a unified voice but tweak taglines for regional resonance.

- **Content and creative:** The hub builds the toolkit—templates, videos, visuals. The spokes personalize. No more rebriefing agencies in fourteen countries.

- **Digital and paid media:** The hub sets the playbook and owns vendor relationships. The spokes tweak targeting and creative for local relevance.

- **Analytics:** Central teams define KPIs and reporting dashboards. Local teams get the data that matters to their region—no more waiting three weeks for HQ to send a spreadsheet.

- **SEO and web:** The hub owns the platform. The spokes own the language. That's how an e-commerce brand wins both Google and customers in twelve languages.

- **PR and communications:** Messaging starts at the center. But stories are told locally. Global headlines don't always matter on the ground—but relevance does.

- **Events and sponsorships:** HQ secures the Super Bowl. Local teams throw the after-party that actually wins customers.

- **CRM and marketing automation:** The hub builds the engine. The spokes steer it with local audience insights, behaviors, and buying cycles.

- **Product marketing:** Central teams launch. Local teams land. No more tone-deaf global campaigns about ski jackets in tropical markets.

- **Social media:** The hub sets the tone. The spokes make it human. Nothing builds brand love like a local reply in your language within five minutes.

The hub-and-spoke model isn't a compromise—it's a design choice. One that recognizes the reality of global marketing today: Structure matters, but so does freedom. The best teams don't fight the model. They fine-tune it. And the result? Brands that scale with soul. Ideas that travel. Work that works—everywhere.

Getting the Hub-and-Spoke Model Right

A hybrid model is one of the hardest marketing transformations to get right. We've seen global brands botch it by overcentralizing, underempowering, or losing sight of who's actually doing the work on the ground.

So, what does it take to shift toward a hub-and-spoke marketing structure that doesn't just look good on paper but performs in-market?

1. **Know who does what:** The hub leads with strategy, brand, budget, and data. The spokes make it real in-market. That's it. Clear roles, clear decisions. No blurred lines.

2. **Collaboration that doesn't die in a deck:** Leadership needs to model cross-team respect. Syncs shouldn't just be updates—they should be knowledge transfers. Build the habit of sharing what's working.

3. **Brand frameworks, not brand prisons:** Global brand consistency should guide, not suffocate. A solid DAM system lets local teams build with confidence.

4. **Shared stack, local smarts:** One martech stack. One data source. But let local teams access what they need, when they need it.

5. **Speed over perfection:** Your structure should flex. The hub sets direction. Spokes test, learn, and move. This isn't a waterfall process— it's jazz.

6. **One set of numbers:** No one wants "their version" of the data. KPIs should ladder up. Dashboards should show global impact and local nuance.

7. **A budget that balances:** Global teams fund big plays. Local teams steer their own spend. Don't make them beg for every banner ad.

8. **Content that travels:** The hub makes templates and playbooks. Spokes tweak, translate, and take it live. No more eighty-slide decks that never leave the inbox.

9. **Talk more; train more:** Quarterly town halls are not enough. Make learning part of the culture. And don't just train down—train across.

10. **Build to adapt:** Your org chart isn't set in stone. It should evolve with tech, behavior, and culture. Build a feedback loop and use it.

Microsoft: Scaling Marketing with a Hub-and-Spoke Model

With operations in more than one hundred countries and a product portfolio spanning cloud services, software, gaming, and hardware, Microsoft faces the constant challenge of delivering consistent brand messaging while staying relevant to diverse global markets. To manage this complexity, Microsoft has adopted a hub-and-spoke marketing model that balances global control with local autonomy.

Microsoft's business operates across multiple verticals and buyer segments, from enterprise to consumer. A one-size-fits-all approach wasn't viable—what resonates in Silicon Valley doesn't always translate in Seoul or São Paulo. The company needed a structure that would align marketing strategy globally while empowering regional teams to execute locally and respond to fast-changing market conditions.

Microsoft implemented a hub-and-spoke marketing organization. Global marketing teams at headquarters own the brand framework, campaign strategy, creative toolkits, and major vendor partnerships. Local marketing teams (the spokes) are responsible for adapting these assets and executing region-specific programs tailored to their market context.

The global marketing team develops centralized messaging platforms—such as those for Azure, Microsoft 365, or Dynamics—along with creative assets and media strategies. These are distributed to regional teams through a shared martech infrastructure, including centralized content libraries and campaign planning tools.

Local teams then translate and adapt content, manage regional media buys, run localized demand generation, and build in-market relationships. Performance data flows both ways, enabling real-time campaign optimization and cross-market learning.

Key takeaways:

- **Structure is strategy:** A hub-and-spoke model isn't just an org chart—it's a way to scale marketing without sacrificing relevance. Define roles clearly: Global leads the "what"; local owns the "how."
- **Local execution needs global enablement:** Central teams should focus on building the toolkit—frameworks, assets, and data systems—that empower local teams to move fast and stay on brand.
- **Invest in shared infrastructure:** A unified martech stack and centralized dashboards aren't nice-to-haves—they're the connective tissue that keeps global and local aligned and accountable.
- **Feedback has to flow both ways:** The best ideas don't always come from HQ. Build channels for bottom-up insight to shape top-down strategy.
- **Don't just protect the brand—activate it:** The hub's job isn't to say no; it's to make yes easier. Give spokes the freedom to adapt messaging while maintaining integrity.
- **Measure what matters at every level:** Create shared KPIs that ladder up from local tactics to global objectives. Everyone should know how their work contributes to the big picture.

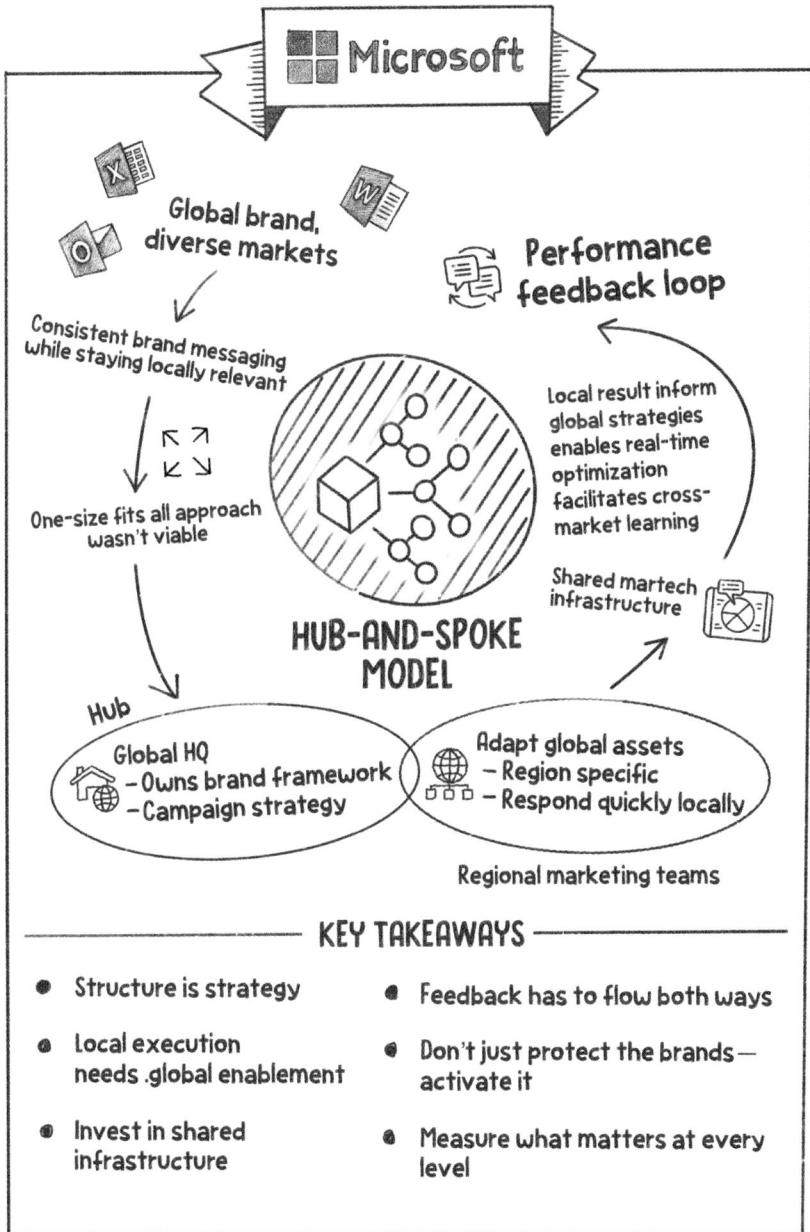

Microsoft

Global brand, diverse markets

Performance feedback loop

Consistent brand messaging while staying locally relevant

Local result inform global strategies enables real-time optimization facilitates cross-market learning

One-size fits all approach wasn't viable

Shared martech infrastructure

HUB-AND-SPOKE MODEL

Hub

Global HQ
- Owns brand framework
- Campaign strategy

Adapt global assets
- Region specific
- Respond quickly locally

Regional marketing teams

——— KEY TAKEAWAYS ———

- Structure is strategy
- Local execution needs .global enablement
- Invest in shared infrastructure

- Feedback has to flow both ways
- Don't just protect the brands — activate it
- Measure what matters at every level

Chapter 3
The Shape of Marketing Teams

In marketing and business operations, the terms *governance* and *operating structures* are often mentioned together—but they serve very different purposes. Governance is about *how decisions are made, evaluated, and enforced.* It includes the systems, rules, and practices that guide how an organization aligns with its strategy and maintains accountability.

Strong governance ensures that even with a solid structure, the right choices are being made. Organizational structure, on the other hand, defines *how work is divided and executed.* It's the formal arrangement of roles, responsibilities, reporting lines, and team configurations. Structure is about *who does what* and *how the work flows.*

You can have a beautifully designed marketing org chart—but without governance, it risks becoming siloed or reactive. Conversely, tight governance without the right structure can stifle creativity and speed.

For modern marketers, success lies in getting both right. Structure gives you *clarity and efficiency*; governance gives you *consistency and control.* The most effective marketing organizations build strong foundations in both, allowing them to scale smarter, respond faster, and deliver work that truly resonates.

"The strategic direction of Coca-Cola requires for us to operate a network model," says Shakir Moin, President, Marketing, North America. "This is not a *command-and-control-out-of-the-centre* structure, or even a *lead market* type of arrangement. It's a network model which leverages the best of multiple markets. It's anchored on data capability and drives connectivity globally."

Common Marketing Operating Structures

To better grasp how marketing teams can be structured to navigate current and future challenges, let's review different organizational models.

- **The Command Tower:** Symbolizes hierarchy, clarity, and control—just as a CEO like Eisenhower or Steve Jobs would lead from the top with strong marketing belief.
- **Web of Collaboration:** Highlights the connectedness and fluid sharing of thinking across teams, like the Goosebumps team at Coca-Cola.
- **Circle of Innovation:** Suggests equality, creativity, and shared ownership—just like the Mars-Nitro example where the CMO cocreated the work.
- **The Galaxy Model:** Represents stars orbiting a common gravity— great for global brands with independent teams bound by a unifying purpose or vision.
- **The Enterprise Grid:** Reflects operational segmentation with a business lens—works well for large companies aligning marketing closely with P&L.
- **The Agile Scrum:** Feels more action oriented, fast moving, and contemporary—matching today's leaner, decentralized, reactive teams.

The Command Tower

There's something deeply comforting about clarity. Like an air traffic controller guiding flights in and out, the Command Tower is where marketing knows exactly who's in charge, what needs to be done, and when it needs to happen. This is the classic pyramid—the structure most CMOs walk into on day one.

At the top of the tower, the CMO stands like a general with a bird's-eye view—crafting strategy, setting priorities, and rallying the troops. Below, a disciplined cascade of vice presidents, directors, managers, and specialists follows. Each layer has a defined purpose. Everyone knows their place. Everyone knows their lane. It's orderly. It's dependable. And for companies with massive scale—think legacy CPGs, global automakers, or conservative financial institutions—it works. When the goal is consistency, control, and risk minimization, this structure hums.

But here's the catch: The view from the top doesn't always reflect what's happening on the ground. We've seen brilliant strategies stall because the feedback loop took too long to travel back up the tower. We've watched creative magic get lost between a director's sign-off and a VP's spreadsheet. And we've seen marketers closer to the customer than the CMO—yet unable to make a call without three levels of approval.

The Command Tower excels at directing traffic. But it's less built for spontaneous collaboration, fast pivots, or bold experimentation. In a world where brands live and die by their ability to move at the speed of culture, some towers start to feel like fortresses. That doesn't mean it's broken. It just means it needs retooling.

Procter & Gamble: The Command Tower in Action

If ever there was a poster child for the Command Tower, it's Procter & Gamble. In a world of over sixty billion-dollar brands, you don't improvise your way to the top. You organize. You systematize. You climb the tower.

At the summit sits the CMO—overseeing an empire of marketing machinery. Below, a battalion of marketing directors leads by category or region, ensuring that every diaper, razor, and detergent follows a disciplined playbook. Brand managers—often MBA-trained, data-savvy operators—execute strategy for individual products. Supporting them are assistants and coordinators who keep the engine humming, analyzing data and managing the day-to-day.

This model is built for scale. It thrives on clarity and command. Everyone knows their lane. No one freelances the Pampers plan.

P&G's multilayered approvals can mean great ideas get stuck in traffic. Brand teams sometimes act like islands—intensely focused on their own KPIs, not the bigger picture. The collaboration that sparks creativity can be hard to come by. Still, there's something to admire in the discipline. In a chaotic marketing world, the Command Tower gives P&G a powerful edge: control.

Benefits and Challenges: The Command Tower

Aspect	Benefits	Challenges
Chain of command	Clear reporting structure reduces confusion and improves accountability.	Slow decision-making can occur due to multiple approval layers.
Decision-making	Leadership enforces consistency and strategic planning effectively.	Bureaucracy can make companies less agile and slow to adapt to market changes.
Specialization and expertise	Employees develop deep expertise within their departments, improving efficiency.	Siloed departments may struggle with cross-functional collaboration.
Stability and predictability	Defined roles and procedures create a stable and organized work environment.	Rigid structure can discourage innovation and adaptability.

Scalability	Expansion is easy with additional managerial layers as the company grows.	Higher levels of management may slow communication and decision-making.
Innovation and employee input	Clear leadership ensures strategic alignment.	Lower-level employees may feel unheard, limiting creative input and engagement.
Dependence on leadership	Strong leadership provides direction and structure.	Poor decision-making at the top can negatively impact the entire organization.
Employee retention	Stable career progression exists within structured roles.	Limited opportunities for rapid promotion can lead to frustration and high turnover.

Web of Collaboration

A matrix organizational model is characterized by collaboration across teams, with team members often reporting to multiple bosses. Key features of this model include enhanced flexibility and adaptability.

Imagine a web rather than a pyramid. In a matrix structure, marketing teams have dual reporting lines. One line connects to a functional manager, such as a content director, who oversees specific expertise areas like writing and design. The other line connects to a product manager responsible for a specific product line, such as smartphones or fitness trackers.

Team members, including copywriters and graphic designers, engage in projects across various products, applying their specialized skills to each campaign. This setup enhances collaboration and enables faster adaptations. For example, a social media specialist can combine expertise with product knowledge to customize campaigns for different products.

However, this setup can also create confusion regarding priorities and workload. Clear communication and strong leadership are crucial to manage these overlapping responsibilities successfully.

"At Glanbia Performance Nutrition, we have a brand growth model that's designed to integrate marketing and sales efforts and identify what we need to have in place to make things happen," says Glanbia's Colin Westcott-Pitt. "Pricing is probably the best example of a joint effort—the marketer should be able to articulate and land the pricing strategy and the sales or commercial team can then execute it."

Philips: Marketing Across the Matrix

Philips, a global player in both healthcare and consumer electronics, doesn't just straddle industries—it straddles complexity. We were fortunate enough to help the company on a global transformation at the height of COVID-19. What we were able to achieve together was a testament to the importance of collaboration across their marketing community and a mindset of always seeking better outcomes, even in the middle of a pandemic.

To thrive in fast-moving, highly regulated, and culturally diverse markets, Philips built a matrix marketing structure that walks the tightrope between global consistency and local relevance.

At the heart are global product managers, each charged with developing strategy for key business lines—consumer lifestyle, healthcare, and lighting. They think big, long term, and category first. On the ground, regional marketing managers execute those strategies in-market—whether that's in Tokyo or Toronto. They bring the nuance, the local insight, the "what actually works here" perspective.

Threading it all together are functional teams—digital, brand, comms—who work horizontally across product lines and regions. These teams don't just connect the dots; they draw new ones, sparking innovation and ensuring campaigns feel both cohesive and customized.

The result? A marketing engine that flexes in all directions. Philips can respond to trends in a single market without veering off its global brand path. However, dual reporting lines mean marketers often answer to two masters—regional and product—creating friction and occasional confusion. And when everyone gets a vote, decisions can stall in endless alignment loops. Still, the matrix works because Philips knows its stakes. Healthcare demands local trust. Consumer tech demands global scale. The matrix gives them both.

Benefits and Challenges: Web of Collaboration

Aspect	Benefits	Challenges
Flexibility and adaptability	Allows companies to quickly adjust to market changes and project needs.	Complex reporting relationships can create confusion and conflicts.
Cross-functional collaboration	Encourages teamwork between different departments, leading to innovation.	Employees may receive conflicting instructions from multiple managers.
Efficient resource allocation	Teams can share resources across projects, reducing duplication of efforts.	Competing priorities may lead to inefficiencies and delays.
Improved communication	Strong communication between departments is promoted, leading to a more integrated organization.	Strong coordination and communication is required to avoid misalignment.
Employee development	Employees gain diverse skills by working on multiple projects across functions.	Heavy workloads and multiple responsibilities can lead to burnout.
Faster decision-making	Decision-making is distributed across multiple leaders rather than centralized.	Managers must be highly skilled to balance authority and prevent confusion.
Customer-centric approach	Specific customer needs can be tailored for by bringing in expertise from multiple teams.	Managing customer expectations across multiple departments can be challenging.
Scalability	This is suitable for large, complex organizations that require a dynamic approach.	More administrative overhead is needed to maintain structure and coordination.

Circle of Innovation

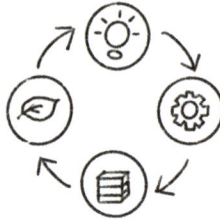

Forget the pyramid. Forget the tower. In some of the most dynamic marketing environments, structure isn't stacked—it's spread. Welcome to the Circle of Innovation.

Here, titles matter less than talent.

Think of a start-up's war room or a scrappy brand's early days. You've got ten people wearing ten hats—strategy, social, creative, analytics—switching gears midconversation. Decisions are made in real time. Campaign leadership isn't assigned by seniority but by who's best for the job. Everyone has a voice, and more importantly, everyone is expected to use it.

There's a catch, of course. When everyone owns the work, no one always owns the outcome. Without crystal-clear goals, strong communication, and rock-solid trust, the web can unravel. Fast.

Gore-Tex: Innovation Without Titles

For W. L. Gore & Associates—the makers of Gore-Tex—structure isn't about climbing a ladder. It's about following the work. From its founding, Gore rejected traditional hierarchies in favor of what it calls a lattice structure—a radically flat, peer-to-peer model that empowers employees to lead without needing a title. In the Web of Innovation model, Gore lives at the center.

There are no formal bosses. Instead, employees—called "associates"—are trusted to build relationships, identify opportunities, and take ownership of their projects. Leadership isn't assigned; it's earned. People naturally follow those with expertise, not job titles.

Here, innovation thrives. Teams form organically around ideas. Associates collaborate across functions, products, and markets without needing permission or passing through layers of management. Gore's marketing teams work this way too—sharing responsibility for campaigns, product storytelling, and customer insights, all grounded in mutual respect and collective accountability. This structure enables a responsiveness and creativity that's difficult to match in more traditional command-and-control companies.

Benefits and Challenges: Circle of Innovation

Aspect	Benefits	Challenges
Decision-making speed	Faster decision-making can occur, as there are fewer layers of management.	Lack of structured leadership can lead to confusion and inefficiencies.
Employee autonomy	Employees are encouraged to take ownership of their work and make independent decisions.	Not all employees thrive in a self-managed environment, leading to potential productivity issues.
Innovation and creativity	Open communication fosters innovation and the free flow of ideas.	Without clear leadership, disagreements may be harder to resolve.
Collaboration and communication	Fewer layers create direct communication between employees and leadership.	Lack of hierarchy can lead to unclear job roles and responsibilities.
Cost efficiency	Overhead costs are reduced by eliminating middle management salaries.	Scaling the organization can be challenging without structured management.
Employee satisfaction and engagement	Employees feel more valued and empowered, leading to higher job satisfaction.	Some employees may struggle with the lack of clear career advancement opportunities.
Customer responsiveness	Quick decision-making enables faster responses to customer needs.	Without clear authority, accountability for customer-related decisions may be unclear.
Scalability	This works well for small companies and start-ups with highly skilled teams.	This can become inefficient as the company grows and needs more structure.

Collaborative Constellation

In this structure, small, cross-functional teams form a decentralized network within the company. Each team is built around a specific goal or initiative—launching a new product, rethinking brand positioning, driving CRM strategy—and is composed of individuals with complementary skills drawn from across the organization. Think product marketing, data, content, digital, comms—all working side by side.

Instead of passing work up and down a chain of command, teams operate with shared ownership. Leadership is often distributed, chosen based on expertise, not title. Communication is constant. Decisions are made in the room—not deferred up a ladder.

This model promotes speed, accountability, and innovation. It works particularly well in fast-paced companies or global brands managing diverse portfolios. But it also comes with challenges. Without clear governance, teams risk duplication of work or strategic misalignment. And when everyone's empowered, it can be unclear who owns what—or who's on the hook when things go sideways.

Still, when done right, the internal networked model unlocks a level of collaboration and creativity that's hard to match. It gives marketers autonomy while staying connected to a larger vision.

IBM: Building a Network from the Inside Out

IBM, a company with over a century of transformation under its belt, knows that staying relevant in the tech world demands more than innovation—it demands reinvention. And in its approach to marketing, IBM has done just that, shifting away from traditional silos to embrace a networked marketing structure built on cross-functional collaboration and strategic flexibility.

At the heart of IBM's model are internal, decentralized teams organized around product lines, services, or specific geographic markets. These teams aren't operating in isolation—they're embedded within a broader business context, working closely with R&D, sales, and product management to ensure that marketing strategy is baked in from the beginning, not bolted on at the end.

What sets IBM apart is that these internal marketing squads function more like nodes in a network than departments in a chart. They form agile units that align around clear goals and execute with autonomy—while still connecting back to a shared global vision. Strategy flows both ways: from headquarters out to the field and from frontline insights back into the core. While IBM does tap into external partners for creative and technical expertise, the power of its network lies in that it empowers internal teams to act quickly, own outcomes, and stay plugged into both the customer and the company mission.

Cathay Pacific: Moving with the World While Speaking to Home

Cathay Pacific doesn't just fly across the globe—it markets that way too. But here's the magic: While many global brands struggle to balance consistency with local relevance, Cathay has managed to feel at home in both the world and Asia.

At the center is a clear brand vision—premium, poised, and emotionally resonant. Cathay isn't just about taking you somewhere; it's about what movement feels like.

"The thing that we realized is that the importance of emotion has really stood out," says General Manager, Brand, Insights and Marketing Communications, Ed Bell. "We've got this number from a 'drivers of choice' analysis. It's driving up to, like, 20% even, even more of decision in certain markets. However, the role of emotion is underreported because not a lot of companies are doing these kinds of studies. If your main source of information on the market is the sales team, you'll probably never hear this kind of thing."

That insight powers everything. But instead of pushing that message out from a single hub, the airline has built what we'd call a Collaborative

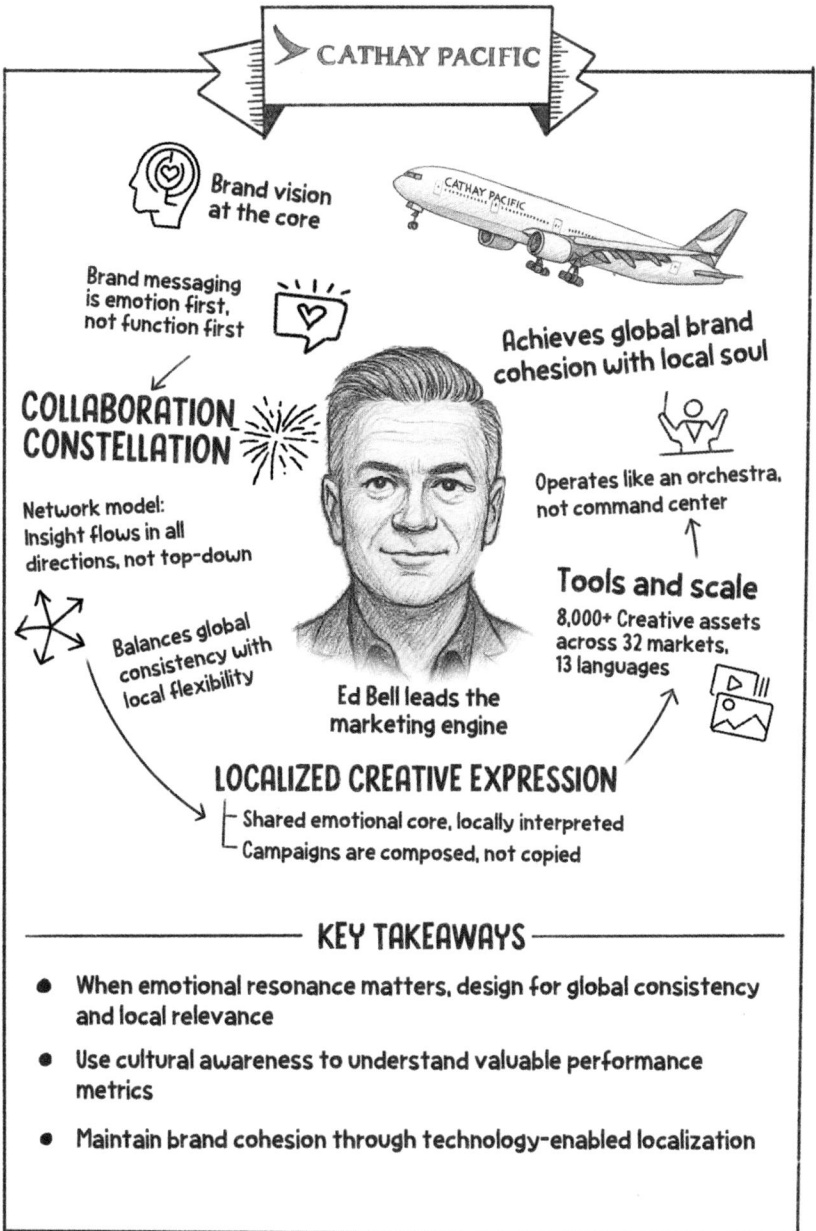

CATHAY PACIFIC

Brand vision at the core

Brand messaging is emotion first, not function first

Achieves global brand cohesion with local soul

COLLABORATION CONSTELLATION

Network model: Insight flows in all directions, not top-down

Operates like an orchestra, not command center

Tools and scale
8,000+ Creative assets across 32 markets, 13 languages

Balances global consistency with local flexibility

Ed Bell leads the marketing engine

LOCALIZED CREATIVE EXPRESSION
├ Shared emotional core, locally interpreted
└ Campaigns are composed, not copied

───────── **KEY TAKEAWAYS** ─────────

- When emotional resonance matters, design for global consistency and local relevance
- Use cultural awareness to understand valuable performance metrics
- Maintain brand cohesion through technology-enabled localization

Constellation—a central team that sets the tone, and regional stars that adapt the light.

Ed Bell leads a marketing engine that doesn't force global uniformity. Instead, it encourages local marketing teams—from Hong Kong to Tokyo to Toronto—to interpret the brand through the lens of local culture. The structure is networked, not hierarchical. Insight doesn't flow just top down—it circulates.

"The Asian business culture prioritises 'tangible.' And I think what happens is that the market is gravitating to performance, because it gives them something tangible," says Ed. "They love influencers. Because they can talk about how many views I got yesterday, yeah, it feels very immediate. It takes away the fear, the fear of the future and the uncertainty of the future."

The result? Campaigns like "Feels Good to Move"—a global platform launched recently—feel universal yet rooted. The core idea is emotional and human. But the storytelling in Tokyo might lean into minimal elegance, while in Bangkok it plays with rhythm and color. The campaign isn't copied—it's composed for each audience.

To pull this off at scale, Cathay doesn't rely on guesswork. Its marketing team uses tech platforms to deliver over eight thousand creative assets across thirty-two markets in thirteen languages. But beyond the tools, it's the insight that matters. Cathay knows that emotional connection drives about 50 percent of consumer choice in its category. And it doesn't just track that—it designs for it.

Global strategy. Local interpretation. Real emotional resonance. Cathay Pacific doesn't just manage its brand—it lets it breathe. That's not easy. That's orchestration. And it's how you build a brand that flies high everywhere while staying grounded in home.

Benefits and Challenges: Collaborative Constellation

Aspect	Benefits	Challenges
Flexibility and adaptability	Allows companies to quickly adapt to changes by leveraging external partnerships.	Managing relationships with multiple external entities can be complex.
Cost efficiency	Reduces overhead costs by outsourcing noncore functions.	Dependence on external partners can lead to risks if they fail to deliver.
Access to specialized talent	Enables organizations to tap into global expertise and specialized skills.	Coordinating different teams and contractors can be challenging.
Scalability	Companies can scale up or down easily by adding or removing external partners.	Quality control becomes difficult when multiple entities are involved.
Innovation and agility	Encourages innovation by bringing in diverse perspectives and expertise.	Communication breakdowns between internal and external teams can slow progress.
Focus on core competencies	Internal teams can focus on strategic goals while outsourcing noncore tasks.	Loss of direct control over outsourced functions may affect performance.
Global reach	Organizations are allowed to operate across different locations without heavy infrastructure investment.	Legal and cultural differences between partners may create complications.
Technology-driven collaboration	Digital tools enable seamless coordination and real-time communication.	Cybersecurity risks increase when dealing with multiple external networks.

The Enterprise Grid

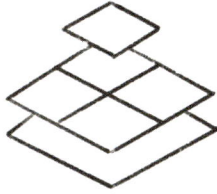

Welcome to the Enterprise Grid—where marketing doesn't live in a single department but across a network of business units, each with its own runway and flight plan. In this model, marketing isn't centralized—it's embedded. Deep inside product lines, regional hubs, customer segments, or verticals, each team operates like its own start-up, but with the backing of a global brand.

This isn't one marketing team trying to be everything to everyone. It's a fleet of speedboats, each engineered for its own mission. The tech division might be pushing SaaS in Singapore, while another is driving loyalty in Latin America. Each has its own CMO, KPIs, budget, and road map. Strategy is tailored. Execution is immediate. Accountability is personal.

But here's the trick: Those boats still need to sail in formation. Without strong brand governance, clear communication, and shared infrastructure—like analytics, media buying, or creative operations—the whole thing veers off course. You get brand inconsistency, duplicated efforts, and the dreaded "fragmentation of the funnel." So while the Enterprise Grid allows each division to move fast and focus deep, the best organizations build connective tissue between the teams to keep the brand intact.

We've seen this model work wonders for companies like Amazon, Microsoft, and GE—each with product and service lines so vast, a single marketing playbook wouldn't cut it. Instead, they empower teams at the edge to market what they know best while still tying everything back to a central brand promise.

L'Oréal: Mastering the Enterprise Grid of Beauty

L'Oréal isn't just a beauty company—it's a beauty empire. And empires need more than a single battle plan. "Digitalization allows access to beauty. Access to education, video content, how to's, the latest looks, and trends," says Asmita Dubey. "Therefore, engagement with beauty automatically keeps on increasing. At L'Oréal we have to be part of that ever evolving conversation."

With a global presence and a product portfolio that stretches from drugstore staples to luxury skin care, L'Oréal has embraced the Enterprise Grid: a divisional marketing structure that lets each business unit write its own playbook—without losing sight of the brand.

At the core of L'Oréal's model are product divisions, each acting as a fully formed marketing engine. Whether it's luxury products, consumer products, professional products, or active cosmetics, each division owns its brand strategy, creative, and go-to-market execution. Marketing teams within these divisions know their customers inside out—whether they're salon professionals, Gen Z skin care fans, or luxury fragrance buyers.

Layered on top of that are regional divisions. From North America to Asia-Pacific, these teams ensure that global campaigns land locally—adjusting messaging, media, and even product lineups based on regional preferences, cultural insights, and beauty trends. In Seoul, skin care reigns. In Paris, prestige leads. And in São Paulo, bold color dominates.

This dual-divisional structure gives L'Oréal a rare advantage: focus and flexibility. It allows teams to move fast, stay close to the customer, and tailor campaigns with surgical precision. But speed comes with trade-offs. With so many teams operating in parallel, resource duplication is a real risk. Without strong brand governance, divisions can drift in tone or miss opportunities to amplify each other's success.

Benefits and Challenges: The Enterprise Grid

Aspect	Benefits	Challenges
Focus on specific markets	Each division operates independently, allowing for tailored strategies for different products, regions, or customer groups.	Divisions may duplicate efforts, leading to inefficiencies and higher operational costs.
Faster decision-making	Decentralized structure enables quicker decision-making within each division.	Lack of coordination between divisions can lead to inconsistencies in company-wide policies.
Clear accountability	Each division has its own leadership, making it easier to track performance and outcomes.	Competition between divisions may create internal conflicts rather than collaboration.
Encourages innovation	Autonomous divisions can experiment with new strategies without affecting the entire company.	Innovation may be limited to specific divisions rather than benefiting the entire organization.
Improved customer service	Customer needs are better addressed, as divisions focus on specific segments or markets.	Customers may experience inconsistent service if divisions operate too independently.
Flexibility and scalability	Expansion can occur by adding new divisions without disrupting the entire company.	Overhead costs can increase due to duplicated roles across divisions (e.g., multiple HR, marketing, or finance teams).
Strong leadership development	Divisional heads gain leadership experience, making it easier to groom future executives.	Highly skilled managers are required who can balance autonomy with alignment to company goals.
Risk management	Problems in one division are less likely to affect the entire company.	If divisions operate too independently, it can weaken the overall company culture and brand identity.

The Agile Scrum

In a world where deadlines are tighter, attention spans shorter, and change constant, traditional marketing models can feel like turning a cargo ship with a teaspoon. That's why more marketing teams are trading long-term planning cycles for the rhythm and rigor of Agile Scrum—a structure borrowed from tech but reengineered for creative problem-solving and speed.

At its core, Agile Scrum is about breaking big challenges into bite-sized sprints. Cross-functional teams—think content creators, data analysts, designers, media planners—come together to tackle a specific marketing goal over a set period (usually two to four weeks). Every morning starts with a stand-up. Every sprint ends with a review. And in between, the team collaborates like a small start-up: focused, fast, and fiercely accountable.

What makes Agile Scrum so powerful in marketing is that it mirrors how modern campaigns actually work. You don't launch once a year. You launch, test, learn, optimize—and then do it again. Agile Scrum gives marketers permission to adapt without starting from scratch, to make smarter decisions in real time, and to cocreate with data rather than guesswork.

But let's be clear—Agile isn't a buzzword. It's a discipline. It requires buy-in from leadership, protection from constant interruption, and trust in the process. When done well, it unlocks autonomy and momentum. When done poorly, it turns into chaos disguised as collaboration.

adidas: Running on Sprints

In the high-speed world of sportswear, timing is everything. Whether it's reacting to a viral trend, launching a collab, or aligning with a global sporting event, adidas knows that winning in the market means moving faster than the competition. That's why the brand has reengineered its marketing engine around an Agile Scrum structure, built for speed, flexibility, and relentless consumer focus.

At the heart of adidas's approach are squads—small, self-organizing teams made up of marketers, designers, analysts, and product managers. Each squad is laser focused on a specific campaign, product, or regional market. They operate like start-ups inside the brand: autonomous, empowered, and accountable for results. No waiting on approvals. No death by PowerPoint. Just fast cycles of ideation, execution, and iteration.

Zoom out, and you'll find tribes—clusters of squads that focus on broader themes like performance, lifestyle, or streetwear. These tribes bring cohesion without killing creativity. They keep squads aligned to the brand's North Star while letting each team own its lane.

Campaigns run in sprints—short, focused bursts of work that deliver tangible outputs, informed by real-time data. Consumer feedback isn't something you gather at the end—it's baked into the process from day one. That allows adidas to pivot quickly, test bold ideas, and get smarter with every launch. With so many squads moving at once, maintaining brand consistency across markets and channels takes serious coordination. And Agile isn't a "set and forget" model—it demands discipline, training, and cultural buy-in to truly work.

Benefits and Challenges: Agile Scrum

Aspect	Benefits	Challenges
Flexibility and adaptability	Rapid responses to market changes, customer needs, and industry trends are enabled.	Frequent changes can create uncertainty and require continuous learning.
Fast decision-making	Teams are empowered to make quick decisions without bureaucratic delays.	Strong leadership is required to ensure alignment across teams.
Innovation and creativity	Experimentation and continuous improvement are encouraged.	It can be difficult to implement in highly regulated industries with strict compliance requirements.
Collaboration and cross-functionality	Teams work across functions, fostering knowledge sharing and problem-solving.	Employees must be highly skilled in multiple areas, which may not always be feasible.
Employee engagement and autonomy	Employees have more ownership over their work, leading to higher motivation and job satisfaction.	Some employees may struggle with the lack of clear hierarchy and direction.
Customer-centric approach	Customer feedback and iterative development are prioritized to improve products and services.	Customer expectations must be managed carefully to avoid constant scope changes.
Efficiency and productivity	This approach eliminates wasteful processes and focuses on delivering value quickly.	Initial implementation can be challenging and may require cultural shifts in the organization.
Scalability	This can be applied across teams and scaled gradually within an organization.	Scaling agility across large enterprises can be complex and requires strong coordination.

Chapter 4
The CMO as Growth Architect

The CMO role is the strangest seat in the C-suite. In some companies, it's been quietly retired, scattered into fragments—chief growth officer, chief experience officer, head of digital. In others, it's the launchpad to CEO. Sometimes the job is about storytelling. Other times, it's about spreadsheets. Some last eighteen months. Some last decades. And once in a while, they make it all the way to the top.

Why the chaos?

It starts with the fact that marketing is still the most misunderstood discipline in business. Ask ten CEOs what their CMO is supposed to do, and you'll get ten different answers: "Drive brand love." "Run ads." "Own the customer." "Deliver revenue." "Fix culture." "Lead innovation." The title hasn't changed, but the expectations have ballooned.

That makes the role structurally unstable. Many are expected to drive growth but don't own pricing, product, e-commerce, or innovation. It's like asking an architect to build a skyscraper without touching steel, concrete, or permits. When expectations and influence don't match, tenure becomes a coin toss. Then there's company culture. At a founder-led tech firm, marketing might be absorbed by product. At a legacy CPG, it's the core engine of value. One company calls it in-house. Another outsources it entirely. One rewards boldness. Another penalizes it. There is no marketing orthodoxy—only context.

And let's be honest: Marketing is a lightning rod. When results stall, the CMO is the first to go. Agency pitch. New logo. New campaign. New CMO. Like clockwork.

But here's the real story: The best marketers don't wait for definition. They create it. They speak the language of the CFO. They collaborate like a COO. They craft purpose with the CHRO. They don't run marketing—they run impact. Morgan Flatley. Raja Rajamannar. Diego Scotti. They didn't inherit power. They built it.

The Scope of Marketing Is Expanding

CMOs are also overseeing AI, commercial, design, innovation, and product capabilities.

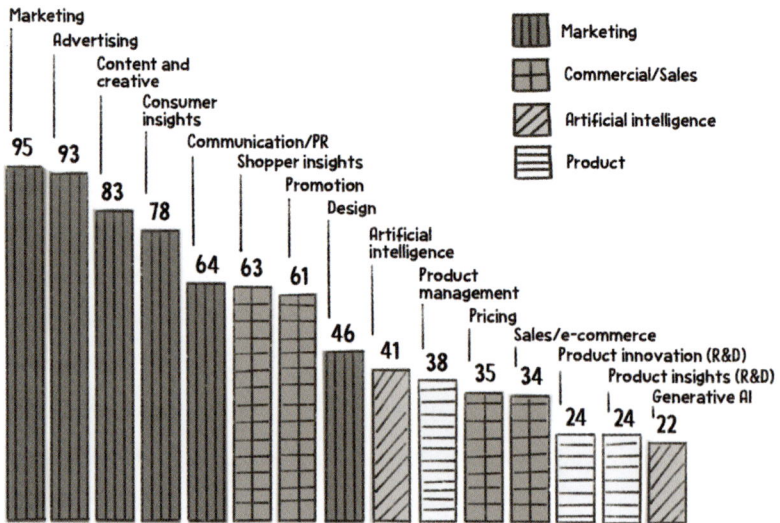

Marketing leaders responsible for each topic, percentage of respondents.

Q: Which of the following are within the remit of the marketing organization (e.g., directly report into the head of the marketing function)? Select all that apply.
Source: McKinsey Global Consumer Marketing Leader Survey, 2024

Building CMO Influence from the Inside

The CMO seat is still the hottest in the C-suite—shorter tenures, higher turnover, and constant scrutiny. According to Spencer Stuart's *CMO Tenure Study*, average tenure sits at 4.2 years, dropping to 3.1 for top advertisers. But here's the twist: 10 percent are now stepping up to CEO roles. The role isn't fading—it's evolving. For those who expand beyond brand into growth, customer, and innovation, the path leads upward. The volatility isn't a sign of weakness—it's a test. The question isn't how long chief marketers stay. It's what they build while they're there.

Those who will lead the next decade aren't waiting to be invited in—they're already at the table, blueprint in hand. Today's top marketers see themselves not as function heads but as architects of growth. They put themselves in the rooms where strategy gets made, not just where campaigns get reviewed.

> *You need to elevate the role of marketing to the highest level in the organization. Marketing must be the day job of a very senior person in the company.*
> **—Mukul Deoras, Colgate-Palmolive**

> *One of the things that I say about the role of a CMO is our key responsibility to also be the Chief Growth Officer. I think so many times CMOs can get distracted by the community, the awards, the creativity. Growth isn't a function . . . it's the mission.*
> **—Emily Ketchen, Lenovo**

> *The very best marketers can talk about the business a credible way. They understand the challenges of the sales or commercial teams. They can then talk even more fully about equity, creative campaigns or other elements of marketing.*
> **—Colin Westcott-Pitt, Glanbia**

A big piece of work for me is educating the company on what marketing is—its purpose, its impact, and what great marketing looks like. While some organizations see marketing as a cost center, I firmly believe that when done right, it becomes a powerful growth engine.
—Eric Lempel, Sony Interactive Entertainment

Consider the case of Diego Scotti, Verizon's former CMO, who was elevated to EVP and now oversees brand, culture, and talent. Or Syl Saller at Diageo, who evolved from global CMO to a board-level presence shaping enterprise transformation. At McDonald's, Morgan Flatley's elevation from US CMO to global CMO and EVP demonstrates that the marketing role is now seen as a business-building engine. "If you look at the history of L'Oréal, marketers have been the growth architects of our company," says Asmita Dubey. "All our CEOs have been marketeers."

These examples speak to a recalibration of what marketing leadership means. CMOs are now expected to do the following:

- Quantify the brand's contribution to valuation.
- Sit alongside CFOs in quarterly earnings strategy.
- Influence product road maps and commercial innovation.
- Serve as public-facing brand stewards in times of crisis.

Four systemic forces are powering this C-suite return:

1. **Data as a common language:** Marketing has embraced quantification, translating creative investments into metrics like net promoter score (NPS), customer lifetime value (CLV), return on marketing investment (ROMI), and growth share. Marketing dashboards now influence earnings calls.

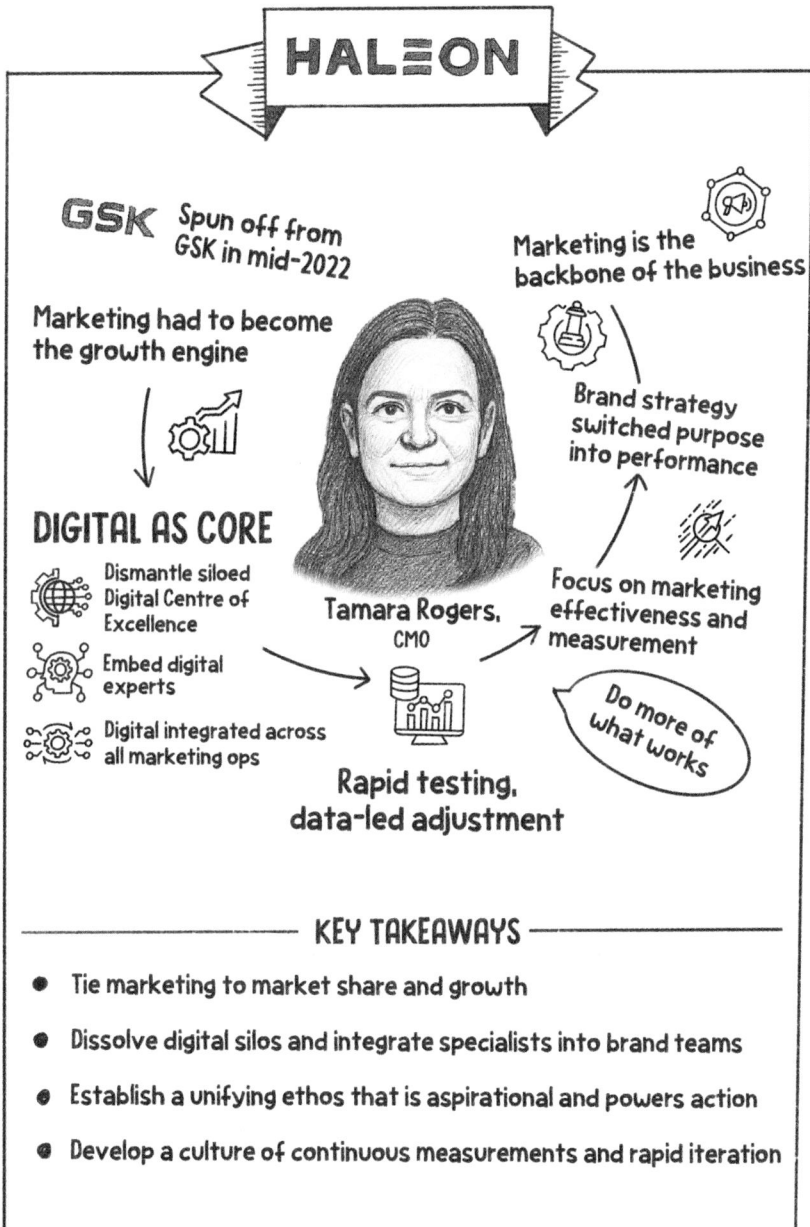

HALEON

GSK Spun off from GSK in mid-2022

Marketing is the backbone of the business

Marketing had to become the growth engine

Brand strategy switched purpose into performance

DIGITAL AS CORE

Dismantle siloed Digital Centre of Excellence

Embed digital experts

Digital integrated across all marketing ops

Tamara Rogers, CMO

Focus on marketing effectiveness and measurement

Do more of what works

Rapid testing, data-led adjustment

─────────── KEY TAKEAWAYS ───────────

- Tie marketing to market share and growth
- Dissolve digital silos and integrate specialists into brand teams
- Establish a unifying ethos that is aspirational and powers action
- Develop a culture of continuous measurements and rapid iteration

2. **Full-spectrum CX:** Marketing owns the end-to-end experience—from ad impression to product delivery to customer advocacy. This horizontal integration has elevated marketers into business integrators.

3. **Societal leadership:** In a polarized world, brands are expected to take stands. CMOs must navigate social tension and purpose alignment with both agility and authenticity.

4. **Financial integration:** Marketing leaders increasingly coauthor quarterly business reviews, scenario plans, and margin improvement road maps. Marketing is now tied to EBITDA.

In short, marketing is no longer outside the tent. It *is* the tent. Look at leaders like Andrea Albright at Walmart, Kristi Argyilan at Albertsons, or Ukonwa Ojo, formerly of Amazon Prime Video. They're not waiting for permission to lead—they're leading from day one. They're not interested in airtime—they're focused on outcomes. "The secret of great marketing is to realize that the battle for the business starts in the mind," says Cathay Pacific's Ed Bell. "At the end of the day, the only reason to have marketing is because it accelerates growth. No one needs marketing to turn the lights on." In response, it's no coincidence that the title itself is changing. Chief growth officer. Chief experience officer. Chief customer officer. These aren't "marketing lite" roles. They're marketing evolved. They reflect a function that now spans revenue, retention, innovation, and impact.

That's the modern leader: half artist, half analyst. Part diplomat, part developer. All in on growth.

The boardroom may still have its gatekeepers, but the best marketers today aren't knocking—they're already inside. Because they understand something too many still miss:

Growth is not a function. It's a mindset.

And marketing, when done right, is growth.

Haleon's CMO Makeover: Rewriting the Marketing Blueprint

When GSK spun off Haleon in mid-2022, the marketing half had to become more than a division—it had to become the heart of a stand-alone growth engine. Enter Tamara Rogers, CMO and former Unilever veteran. In her first move, she made clear this wasn't marketing as usual: "I will be judged on our market share. It's a clear signal of performance," she told *Marketing Week*.

Rogers started with structure over spectacle. She dismantled a siloed digital center of excellence and embedded digital experts into every brand squad. At the same time, she sharpened the lens on marketing effectiveness: rigorous measurement, rapid cycles of "do more of what works," and everyday tweaks that stitched purpose into performance.

Brand came alive through purpose. Rogers rallied her nine power brands around a shared ethos—"better everyday health with humanity." Theraflu's Right to Rest & Recover fund, a tie-up addressing paid sick leave, became a tangible example of purpose-driven action tied to strategy. On the rebrand front, Rogers led a global identity overhaul—from name and logo to sonic branding. Testing 2,050 name options, she landed on "Haleon"—a fusion of "hale" and "leon"—fortified with dynamic green visual cues and a live-sung corporate sonic identity that featured employee voices.

And the results speak volumes. Embedded digital, sharpened metrics, purpose-led brand activism—Rogers didn't just evolve marketing; she built the business's backbone. In Marketing Inside terms, she didn't paint the walls—she built the house. And in the process, she redefined what enterprise-level marketing leadership really looks like.

Key takeaways:

- Tie marketing to market share and growth.
- Dissolve digital silos and integrate specialists into brand teams.
- Establish a unifying ethos that is aspirational and powers tangible actions.
- Develop a culture of continuous measurement and rapid iteration.

Marketing as a Service (MaaS)

I'm going to proffer a new idea called marketing as a service (MaaS). It's an idea that reframes brand building from message delivery to service delivery. It's a direct response to a consumer environment saturated with content and skeptical of overt advertising. To be honest, I stole it from something Keith Weed, former CMO of Unilever, said at a conference recently: "For one hundred years, we were marketing TO people. With the growth of social media, we are now marketing AT people. But to succeed in the future, we need to be marketing FOR people."

My all-time favorite example is Johnson & Johnson's BabyCenter: Think about the moment a woman gets pregnant—the questions she and her partner have, the challenges they have to go through. The fear of the unknown. What if there was a community where ideas could be shared, experiences interchanged, and learning takes place? Beyond content, it provides planning tools, personalized guidance, and community support. It's a trusted companion across the parenting journey. The trust Johnson & Johnson earns translates into brand preference across multiple product lines.

Here are several other great examples:

Nike—Nike+ Ecosystem

Nike+ evolved into a digital fitness and commerce platform offering personalized workouts, community features, and product access. It's MaaS in action: loyalty, CRM, content, and commerce, all wrapped into one.

Adobe—Creative Cloud for Teams

Adobe turned software into service, but its marketing arm did too: Branded education (Adobe Live), marketplace integrations, and creator enablement make it a B2B2C MaaS pioneer.

Starbucks—Deep Personalization Engine

Starbucks uses AI and mobile data to deliver over four hundred thousand variants of personalized offers daily. Its loyalty and CRM stack is offered as a playbook to partners—MaaS disguised as coffee.

Sephora—Virtual Artist Platform

Sephora's AR-based try-on tool became a marketing utility across owned and partner platforms. It's experience as a service, layered with data capture and personalized product conversion.

HubSpot—Content and CRM Suite

HubSpot made inbound marketing into a full-stack, modular system: blogs, lead capture, email flows, CRM. It democratized marketing infrastructure for SMBs—classic SaaS as MaaS.

Amazon—Alexa Voice Marketing

Brands can build "skills" on Alexa. Think of it as voice marketing as a service: open API, on-demand utility, and brand integration in a new medium (e.g., Tide's laundry tips skill).

LEGO—Ideas Platform

LEGO empowers fans to submit and vote on product concepts. Winning ideas get produced, and the creator gets royalties—crowdsourced R&D and community as a service.

Spotify—Wrapped and Fan Insights

Spotify Wrapped isn't just a campaign—it's a data-powered, repeatable marketing experience. Artists now get personalized dashboards too—turning user data into viral, cobranded storytelling.

Airbnb—Neighborhood Guides

Airbnb created location-based travel content layered over its booking engine. Local discovery and trust-building tools became a marketing moat: scalable content plus UX equals marketing utility.

Peloton—Influencer Instructor Network

Peloton's instructors became brand ambassadors, content creators, and CRM drivers. Its entire marketing function flows through a modular stack of community, content, and live programming.

Glossier—Community as a Channel

Glossier scaled by using Slack, Instagram DMs, and community meetups as growth platforms. It turned marketing into a participatory product, letting customers cocreate content and campaigns.

Tesla—Zero-Media Marketing

Tesla built a direct digital funnel—no paid media. Owners evangelize, mobile apps upsell, over-the-air updates retain. A verticalized, self-sustaining MaaS model with built-in network effects.

McDonald's—Dynamic Outdoor Menus

Using weather, time of day, and inventory data, McDonald's outdoor screens update in real time—showing hot coffee on cold mornings or ice cream on hot days. Context as a service.

Coca-Cola—Freestyle Machines

Coca-Cola Freestyle machines deliver data on flavor mixes and frequency—feeding back into new product development, promotions, and retail planning. Physical touchpoints as data-driven media.

IKEA—Planning Tools and Space Creators

IKEA's 3D kitchen and room planners turn product browsing into a service experience. These tools boost basket size and embed the brand into customers' workflows—utility equals conversion.

What It Takes to Deliver MaaS

To deliver MaaS, today's leaders must stop thinking like a campaign manager and start acting like a platform architect. MaaS isn't just a concept—it's a mindset shift. It's the idea that the best marketing is more than theory. It's the foundation for a new approach that sees marketing as embedded utility, not peripheral promotion. Those who get this right won't just run departments. They'll build branded ecosystems that serve, scale, and sell—without ever shouting. Marketing becomes the experience. The product. The reason to stay.

1. **Think like a product manager:** Try to design marketing that solves real problems. Not just content but tools, platforms, and services—like Johnson & Johnson's BabyCenter or Nike Training Club. It's about creating embedded utility, not interruptive messaging.

2. **Frame marketing as a shared enterprise function:** Marketing must operate like an internal service bureau. That means building capabilities—creative, insights, tech, and content—that other departments (product, sales, HR) can leverage to engage customers, employees, and partners alike.

    "Our strategy has three strategic pillars that ensure we deliver business value in everything we do: Build the brand, fuel the business, and create competitive advantage," says Mastercard's Cheryl Guerin. "Each pillar drives specific value back to Mastercard's business and our partners. When we build brand platforms and assets we do so in a way that can be delivered through our partners and customized to meet their needs. Our priceless experiences platform for instance is distributed through partners all around the world in a way that meets their specific objectives and needs."

3. **Invest in the right infrastructure:** MaaS requires scalable tech stacks: CRM, content engines, personalization tools, and AI-powered insight hubs. Build for reuse, not just reach.

4. **Master the metrics:** Measuring ROI for these initiatives becomes a more nuanced and thoughtful discussion. It's not just about the business outcomes but a more diverse set of KPIs depending on the final execution: increased brand dwell time, greater data collection, deeper emotional connection, and higher NPS and lifetime value. Define and defend ROI beyond the media plan.

   > *"Whenever we have a marketing meeting, we start with a business performance discussion," says Glanbia's Colin Westcott-Pitt. "You ground everything there, and then you say, 'What are we doing to help accelerate that business performance and that growth trajectory?'"*

5. **Partner across functions:** The best MaaS strategies are cross-functional—cocreated with IT, CX, and innovation teams. Lead with influence, not just spend.

6. **Embed marketing in the customer journey:** MaaS means showing up before, during, and after the transaction. It's not about the funnel. It's about the relationship—sustained, contextual, and valuable.

Make Marketing Matter

To become a true growth architect, the best leaders will have Marketing Mix Modeling (MMM) within their Swiss Army collection. A good MMM is the closest thing to marketing's Rosetta Stone: a quantitative decoder that translates creative inputs into business outputs. The rise of AI, machine learning, and advanced econometrics has revolutionized MMM's scope, accessibility, and speed.

We've always said that, just like our own services, MMM is not going to *remove* the risk of marketing; it will only help *reduce* it. When paired with attribution and brand equity tracking, MMM becomes a strategic cockpit. It empowers marketers not only to defend their budgets but to grow them. MMM is a source of confidence, not compliance. It allows you to enter budget reviews with authority: "This quarter, social spend outperformed TV by 23 percent, but only in markets with influencer overlay." In a world of infinite tactics, MMM offers strategic clarity. It is not the death of creativity—it's the blueprint for smarter storytelling.

With that important context, finding the optimal solution has never been more important.

MMM in Asia Versus the West

In markets like India or Indonesia, MMM is now being layered with geospatial modeling and offline attribution. CPG companies in these regions use it to understand the interplay between in-store promotion and digital impressions.

At the same time, market maturity will drive a lot of the outcomes of MMM. Procter & Gamble found that in developing markets, marketing is sometimes only the sixth- or seventh-level function in terms of predicting results—and that point of purchase, pricing, and other factors will rise to the top. I still remember ten years ago helping Coca-Cola with MMM in China. Of course, price was the number one criterion on purchase intent—but the number two? That was *weather.* Yes, of course! Hot day? Sell Coke. Cold day? Sell less Coke. Even the most advanced mix models need to take some common sense into account.

Overcoming Short-Termism

A growing concern is that performance marketing overshadows brand building. MMM helps balance this. For example, Diageo's MMM models show how brand campaigns impact purchase intent over six to eighteen months, while promotional bursts affect immediate sales. This helps defend long-term investments. Too often, there's a drive for immediate outcomes, and it's essential that this is balanced with more sensible planning. No CEO is going to survive by constantly missing quarterly projections—but at least building a better understanding of what works and what doesn't work is going to be crucial to the best outcomes.

> *Data has and continues to transform our craft. I fear that the focus on short-term conversion has led to a shortage of those who know what makes a brand a brand and how to build it—an area for capability build. And of course, critically, how do we do that in this new, fragmented, consumer in charge world?*
> *—Tamara Rogers, Haleon*

> *Everyone knows that marketing and brand is important, but the question is, how important? The second part of that sentence is the quantitative question. The first part of it is qualitative—yes, it's important. So how much should we invest if I want to get to a number? How can I rely on my equipment to get to that number? The challenge is bridging the gap between the marathon at the top of the funnel and the sprint at the bottom. If you only do one or the other, the outcome is not going to be optimal.*
> *—Edward Bell, Cathay Pacific*

What It Takes to Deliver MMM

Marketing Mix Modeling used to be the domain of data wonks and postmortem meetings. Annual, expensive, backward looking. Useful—if you didn't mind being too late. But today's MMM? It's fast, dynamic, democratized. It's not just informing marketing culture—it's redefining it. MMM is helping kill gut-led silos and campaign theater. It's empowering marketers to defend long-term brand spend in a world obsessed with short-term clicks. It's aligning teams across functions, bringing finance and marketing into the same room—with the same truth.

Bottom line: MMM isn't killing creativity. It's giving it a business case. And the marketers who master it? They're not just executing. They're orchestrating.

Here are the five shifts that matter:

1. **Always-on calibration:** MMM isn't a once-a-year diagnostic anymore. Monthly refreshes and rolling models mean marketers can react in real time. The model doesn't gather dust—it *learns*.

2. **Scenario planning, not just reporting:** Modern MMM lets teams simulate spend shifts, predict outcomes, and optimize before pulling the trigger. It's a cockpit, not a rearview mirror.

3. **Creative diagnostics:** It's not just channel mix. Today's MMM can evaluate which copy, formats, or influencer executions actually move the needle. Creativity meets accountability.

4. **Financial fluency:** MMM now speaks the language of EBITDA, payback periods, and margin impact. Marketers are now entering budget meetings not with charts but with confidence.

5. **Organizational literacy:** MMM isn't just for analysts anymore. Brand managers, media leads, even finance teams are reading from the same playbook. Shared data equals shared decisions.

Igniting Culture-Driven Marketing

Let's be honest—no one wakes up in the morning hoping to see your ad. But they do wake up plugged into culture. Scrolling, streaming, searching. "I think we've reached a point where we're such a force in entertainment that our competition is now mainstream entertainment," says Eric Lempel of Sony Interactive Entertainment. "Today it's more about whether someone chooses to stream a movie or do something else instead of using their PlayStation."

The brands that matter are the ones that show up—in the conversation, not just on the media plan. "When we get marketing right, we find that consumers are very willing to take in our messages and, in some cases, amplify those messages," continues Lempel. "It's all about respecting their perspective and recognizing that your brand and products aren't the only thing they think about."

Culture-first marketing isn't a trend. It's the new ROI. And for CMOs, it's not just a tactic—it's a growth engine. Because here's the truth: Attention is earned, not bought. When e.l.f. turned a TikTok sound into a Gen Z anthem, it didn't just win impressions—it won advocates. When McDonald's launched celebrity meals with BTS and Travis Scott, it wasn't endorsement—it was cocreation. Sales spiked. Culture moved.

Culture-first marketing does three things brilliantly:

1. **Drives relevance:** You're not shouting into the void; you're part of the moment. That creates emotional connection that no CPM (cost per mille) ever will.

2. **Accelerates reach organically:** When culture shares your story for you, you're not paying for every eyeball. That's media efficiency with brand amplification.

3. **Builds long-term equity:** It's not just buzz. Done right, it deepens identity. Think Patagonia, Ben & Jerry's, Barbie.

> *Culture moves at lightning speed, and so must we. From the Oscars red carpet to the metaverse of Minecraft, L'Oréal is at the forefront of cultural conversation. We're amplifying authentic voices. Our network of 70,000 influencers builds trust and fosters genuine connections with consumers. Today, we co-create with influencers who are makeup artists, who are hairstylists, who are prescribers, advocates, professionals, thousands and thousands of people who are talking to the consumer, and the consumers trust them because of their authenticity.*
> *—Asmita Dubey, L'Oréal*

However, not every brand should be doing culture-first marketing. That's not gatekeeping—it's just honesty. Culture-first marketing only works when a brand has something real to say *and* the right to say it. It's not about tweeting during the Super Bowl or slapping slang on a billboard. If your brand doesn't know who it is, why it matters, or who it's for—culture will chew you up and scroll right past.

The truth? Culture moves fast. If your approval chain takes two weeks and twelve signatures, this game isn't for you. If your marketing team doesn't reflect the culture you're trying to enter, you're just guessing. And if your growth strategy lives and dies on return on ad spend (ROAS), chasing culture might leave you broke *and* ignored.

But if you've got a clear voice, the agility to act, and something *worth* adding to the conversation—then culture-first marketing isn't just a good fit; it's a growth accelerator. The best brands in culture don't try to hijack it. They *contribute* to it. They show up not to sell but to serve. And when they do it right? They don't go viral. They go *vital*.

What It Takes to Deliver Culture-Driven Marketing

Culture-first marketing isn't about chasing hashtags or jumping on every meme. It's about embedding your brand where people actually are—emotionally, socially, and yes, even politically. If your marketing still waits for quarterly briefs, you're already late.

So what does a real leader need to be or do?

- **Be fluent, not trendy:** Cultural relevance isn't about being cool. It's about being fluent in the values, voices, and vernacular of your audience. That means hiring people who live in the culture, not just talk about it. That means listening more than posting.
- **Build in-house speed:** Culture doesn't wait for approval rounds. The new world needs agile teams with permission to act. Think real-time content, social creative pods, and embedded community leads. This isn't campaign mode—it's constant motion.

- **Shift from messaging to meaning:** Ask yourself, "Why would anyone care?" Culture-first brands don't just say something—they stand for something. Purpose isn't a slide—it's an operating system. Just ask Patagonia.

- **Cocreate; don't just curate:** The best cultural marketing is built with the community, not for it. Invite creators in. Collaborate; don't commission. When people see themselves in your brand, they'll carry it further than any media buy.

- **Measure more than clicks:** New KPIs matter: brand mentions, community engagement, cultural momentum. If your only metric is ROAS, you're missing the forest for the fandom.

e.l.f. Beauty: How a CMO Turned a Drugstore Brand into a Cultural Juggernaut

In 2019, e.l.f. was a drugstore staple with low prices and modest buzz. Fast-forward to today, and it's one of the fastest-growing beauty brands in the United States, crossing $1 billion in net sales for the first time—a 77 percent year-over-year increase. The architect behind this rise? CMO Kory Marchisotto.

When Marchisotto arrived, she didn't just refresh the brand—she redefined its entire playbook. Her first move was to go all-in on culture. While legacy beauty brands clung to Instagram aesthetics, e.l.f. dived headfirst into TikTok. Its breakout campaign "Eyes. Lips. Face." in 2019 wasn't an ad—it was a cultural event. With over seven billion views, it became the most viral campaign in TikTok history at the time—and 100 percent organic before a single dollar was spent on media.

Marchisotto turned creators into collaborators and fans into brand builders. e.l.f. was one of the first beauty brands on Twitch, launched branded collabs with Chipotle and Dunkin', and leaned into Gen Z humor, inclusivity, and audacity. These weren't stunts—they were signals: e.l.f. was listening, participating, and leading.

The results? Since 2020, e.l.f. has grown revenue by over 250 percent. This

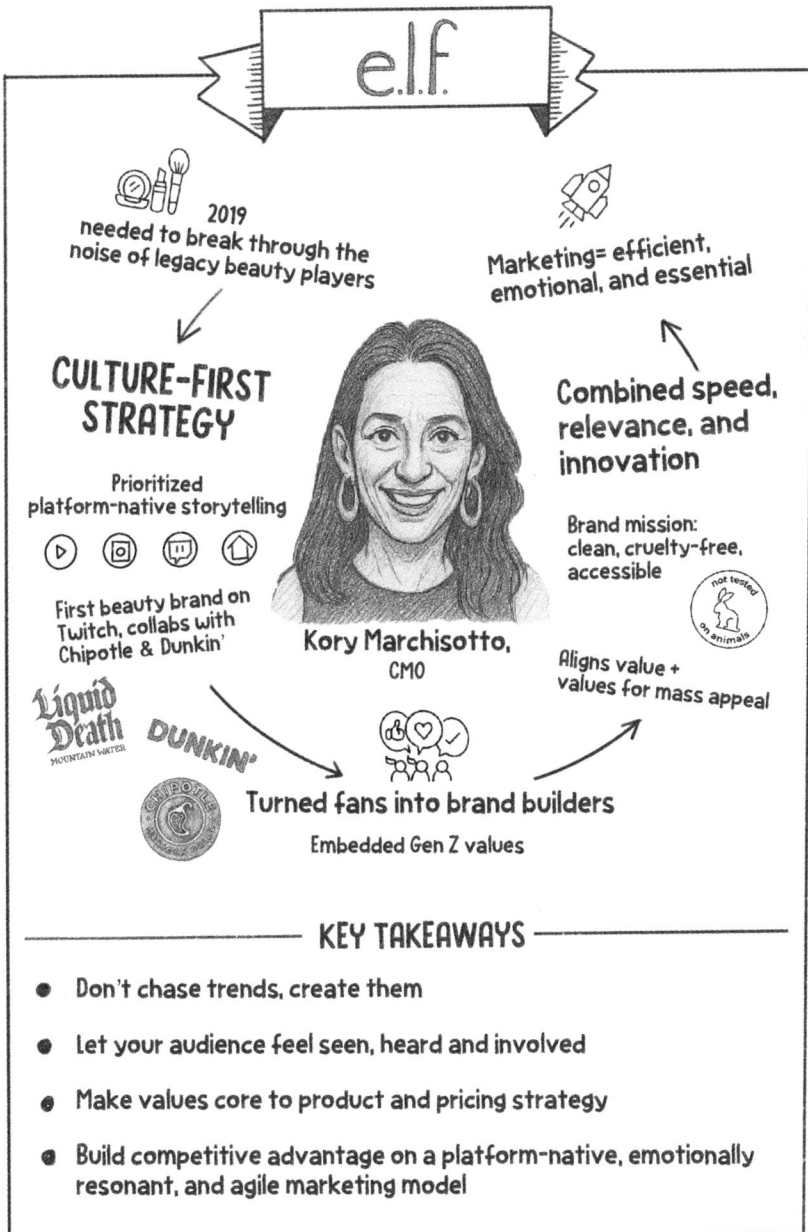

e.l.f.

2019
needed to break through the
noise of legacy beauty players

Marketing= efficient,
emotional, and essential

CULTURE-FIRST STRATEGY

Prioritized
platform-native storytelling

Combined speed,
relevance, and
innovation

Brand mission:
clean, cruelty-free,
accessible

not tested on animals

First beauty brand on
Twitch, collabs with
Chipotle & Dunkin'

Kory Marchisotto,
CMO

Aligns value +
values for mass appeal

Liquid Death
MOUNTAIN WATER

DUNKIN'

CHIPOTLE

Turned fans into brand builders

Embedded Gen Z values

KEY TAKEAWAYS

- Don't chase trends, create them

- Let your audience feel seen, heard and involved

- Make values core to product and pricing strategy

- Build competitive advantage on a platform-native, emotionally resonant, and agile marketing model year alone, the company added over $400 million in sales, expanded into new international markets, and grew digital penetration to 25 percent of total revenue. It's now the number one mass cosmetics brand in the United States in terms of unit sales, beating out giants like L'Oréal and Maybelline.

But Marchisotto didn't just ride a trend—she built a brand that stood for something. e.l.f.'s "clean, cruelty-free, and accessible" mission isn't just copy—it's business strategy. Its nine-dollar Holy Hydration! moisturizer now competes head to head with prestige brands at five times the price. And its Gen Z fanbase? Fiercely loyal. Culturally engaged. Always watching.

In a category known for high spend, e.l.f. flipped the script. Culture-first marketing, platform-native content, and product innovation at speed. Marchisotto made marketing efficient, emotional, and indispensable. This wasn't just a turnaround. It was a takeoff.

Key takeaways:

- Don't chase trends—create them.
- Let your audience feel seen, heard, and involved.
- Make values core to product and pricing strategy.
- Build competitive advantage on a platform-native, emotionally resonant, and agile marketing model.

Venture Builder

One of the most significant shifts is the expectation that marketing doesn't just grow brands—it creates businesses. As companies seek to incubate new revenue streams, marketing leaders are increasingly at the center of internal venture building and innovation. No longer limited to packaging and promotion, today's CMOs are often tasked with conceiving, funding, and launching entirely new business models. In many companies, this means leading in-house innovation studios or DTC (direct-to-consumer) spinouts. In others, it means collaborating with incubators, tech partners, or M&A teams to build proprietary ecosystems.

Here are some cases in point:

- **AB InBev's ZX Ventures.** This global growth and innovation group was built as an autonomous unit reporting directly to the CEO—but led by marketing strategists. It has launched successful brands like Babe Wine and invested in technology start-ups, consumer platforms, and beverage delivery services. ZX Ventures is a blueprint for how to incubate scalable, stand-alone ventures within legacy companies.

- **Unilever Foundry and LEVEL3** (its start-up hub in Singapore) have similarly provided a proving ground for digital ventures and brand extensions. From personalized nutrition to sustainable packaging pilots, Unilever's marketers have partnered with start-ups to bring agile, scalable products to life—faster than traditional brand cycles would allow.

- **PepsiCo's Hive** division operates like a venture capital team inside a food conglomerate. Its portfolio includes health-forward snack brands, sustainable protein products, and lifestyle drinks that reflect emerging consumer behaviors. Marketing insights directly shape product-market fit.

Why the Shift from Brand to Business?

A marketing leader is uniquely positioned to be the venture builder within the business—not because they own the brand but because they own *the signal*.

- **They live closest to the consumer:** No other C-suite role spends more time obsessing over unmet needs, shifting behaviors, and cultural white space. Be the antennae of the organization—constantly tuned in to what's next. That's the starting line for any new venture.
- **They blend creativity with commerciality:** The best know how to shape ideas and how to sell them. They bring together the irrational magic of insight with the rational rigor of go-to-market. That makes them dangerous—in the best way possible.
- **They know how to orchestrate cross-functional teams:** Building a new business inside a big one means working across legal, product, finance, supply chain, and tech. Leaders are already used to running cross-functional war rooms. They can herd cats and get them to dance.
- **They're not afraid of the blank page:** We launch things for a living. Campaigns, brands, platforms, partnerships. Venture building is just a bigger, riskier, more interesting version of the same instinct: Make something new that people want.
- **They can de-risk with brand trust:** New ventures are fragile. The right leader can launch a DTC brand or an innovation line and borrow equity from the parent brand—giving the venture early credibility, distribution, and traction others can't match.

Mondelēz: When the CMO Becomes a Builder, Not Just a Brand Boss

You don't expect a hundred-year-old snack company to act like a start-up. But under the leadership of Chief Marketing and Sales Officer Martin Renaud, that's exactly what Mondelēz has done. Because while most CMOs were still optimizing media plans, Renaud was quietly building something bigger: a pipeline of new ventures inside a legacy machine.

Renaud didn't just talk about innovation—he operationalized it. He championed the launch of SnackFutures, Mondelēz's in-house venture hub, designed not for brand refreshes but for new business creation. The brief? Spot consumer shifts early, test fast, scale what sticks. The team was small, agile, and intentionally scrappy—everything the core business wasn't.

From this engine came Hu Kitchen, a clean-label snacking brand the company fully acquired after early venture success. Véa and Good Thins entered the world as better-for-you snack platforms backed by real behavioral insights, not just trend decks. And through SnackFutures, Mondelēz launched CoLab, a start-up accelerator connecting the company with emerging food entrepreneurs—essentially turning Mondelēz into a scaled innovation eco-system, not just a snacking giant.

Renaud knew that to build the future, you couldn't rely on brand equity alone. You had to earn your way into new categories, new formats, and new behaviors. That meant getting comfortable with ambiguity, fast failure, and unbranded experiments. It also meant empowering teams to operate outside the usual P&L constraints—because growth-stage thinking doesn't fit in a quarterly box.

And while the initiatives were lean, the impact was real. Venture-led innovation contributed to Mondelēz's annual revenue growth of 14 percent, outpacing category benchmarks and proving that *legacy* doesn't mean *lethargic*. Martin Renaud's playbook wasn't about making Oreos more famous. It was about building what comes *after* Oreos. And that's what the best are doing now—not just telling the brand story but writing the next chapter of the business. From the inside.

So You Want to Be a Venture Builder? Read This First.

There's a reason most internal ventures never make it past year one. And it's not the idea—it's the org chart.

Those who step into the venture-builder role need to understand one thing quickly: Your biggest enemy isn't market rejection. It's *internal resistance*. Legacy systems, slow approvals, jealous P&Ls, and brand safety paranoia can kill even the sharpest innovation before it breathes.

The first challenge? **Governance.** You'll be told you have freedom—until legal, finance, and supply chain each ask for "just one approval" before launch. Suddenly your sprint looks like a stumble. The fix? Create a growth board— like a venture capital model—where you pitch for funding and air cover. Set the rules early, and hold the business to them.

Second challenge? **Talent mismatch.** The team that's brilliant at managing mature brands may not be wired to build something from zero. You need start-up DNA—builders, hackers, generalists. And you have to protect them. Nothing kills momentum like matrix meetings with seven vice presidents.

Third? **Performance pressure.** Everyone loves innovation—until it misses a target. Remember, new ventures aren't designed to deliver quarterly ROI. They're built to test, learn, and pivot. Set the right KPIs—signal strength, engagement velocity, early-adopter retention—not just revenue on day one.

Fourth? **Brand friction.** Your new venture might challenge the mother brand's tone, audience, or pricing. Good. That means it's doing its job. But be ready for pushback. You'll need to educate stakeholders on brand stretch, cannibalization myths, and the role of experimentation in brand evolution.

And last? **Short-termism.** We already fight this in campaign land. In venture land, it's worse. Resist the pressure to polish too early. MVP doesn't mean "minimum embarrassment"—it means *maximum learning*.

While internal ventures can fail, the lessons are valuable. Brands like Coca-Cola's Honest Tea and McDonald's McPlant line were born from lean experimentation. The marketing teams behind them used real-world feedback loops to iterate offerings that complemented the core business. According to a recent Bain report, companies with innovation boards saw 1.7 times faster go-to-market rates and a 35 percent higher success rate in new product launches.

This shift toward venture-minded marketing represents more than agility—it's a fundamental redefinition of what it means to drive growth.

AI: Growth's New Operating System

AI is the scaffolding of modern growth. And if you aren't leading that transformation, someone else will—likely the CTO, CFO, or some external consultant with a dashboard and a buzzword list. But make no mistake: The CMO is uniquely positioned to own AI. Why? Because no one else in the building sits at the intersection of customer need, data insight, and brand ambition. AI isn't just about automation—it's about anticipation. And marketers live on that edge every day.

A great CMO understands that AI isn't a replacement for creativity; it's an accelerant. With the right models, you don't just generate content faster—you generate smarter segments, personalized journeys, dynamic pricing strategies, and product ideas grounded in real-time behavior. You don't market to personas. You market to people.

The business case? Crystal clear. AI unlocks speed, scale, and precision. Brands using AI in media optimization are seeing up to 30 percent improvements in ROI. CRM teams are doubling email-open rates with predictive timing. E-comm brands are improving basket size with recommendation engines that adapt in real time.

But here's the bigger point: AI is rewriting how marketing operates. No more static calendars. No more one-size-fits-all campaigns. The marketing head must now lead a shift to continuous learning loops—where creative, data, and performance live in constant dialogue. That requires new tools, yes—but more importantly, it requires new teams, new workflows, and new thinking.

This is not an IT function. It's a growth function. And that means stop waiting for AI strategy to come from the outside. You must own it. Architect it. Scale it.

Leading the Marketing Organization Across a Road Yet Traveled

Everyone wants to talk about AI like it's magic. Smarter targeting. Endless content. Infinite scale. And sure, it *can* be all that, but for most right now, it's mostly PowerPoint and pilot projects. Why? Because the biggest AI challenge isn't the tech—it's the *transformation*. CMOs must lead not just the implementation but the mindset shift that goes with it. Otherwise, AI won't feel like a revolution. It'll feel like another tool we forgot how to use.

However, let's not fool ourselves. There's plenty standing in the way to leveraging AI's potential in marketing.

Let's start with the obvious: **AI needs clean, connected data.** Most marketing teams are still juggling CRM systems built in 2011, media data from six agencies, and e-comm insights stuck in a spreadsheet. You can't train intelligence on chaos. Brands need to *own* the data agenda—not delegate it. Build alliances with your CTO. Create shared dashboards. Make data hygiene a quarterly KPI.

Then there's **talent**. You can't bolt AI onto a 1990s team structure. Marketers now need to sit beside data scientists, prompt engineers, and yes—creatives who know how to work with machines, not fear them. Your job? Build blended squads. Upskill your stars. Bring in specialists who understand both the model and the message.

Next challenge: the brand. AI can generate a thousand headlines, but not all of them should see the light of day. We must **draw the line between personalization and parody**. Create brand-safe AI playbooks. Approve prompt libraries. And most importantly—keep a human in the loop.

And let's not forget the **pressure**. AI doesn't deliver breakthrough ROI on day one. It learns. Slowly. Iteratively. The smart leader doesn't promise magic. They set expectations. Test in controlled environments. Share early wins in language the CFO understands—like margin lift, lead conversion, or CAC reduction.

What It Takes to Lead AI Marketing Transformation

For a CMO to lead AI transformation—not just survive it—they need to evolve from brand steward to systems thinker. This isn't just about understanding what AI does. It's about reshaping how marketing works.

- **No more "I'm not a data person."** The modern marketer must understand data architecture, customer pipelines, and measurement frameworks. You don't need to write code—but you do need to know the difference between structured and unstructured data, what a training set is, and why model bias matters. Speak the language, or you'll get sidelined.

- **Understand the tools.** From CDPs and DMPs to MLOps platforms and Gen AI interfaces. Know what your martech stack can and can't do—and how to stitch it together for insight, activation, and automation. You're not just buying tech. You're designing the engine.

- **AI is not a solo act.** You'll need tight partnerships with IT, product, legal, finance, and customer experience. Build cross-functional squads that can move fast and speak both brand and back end. Influence horizontally.

- **Creative direction in a machine world:** AI can generate content at scale, but it still needs human intent and taste. Define creative standards, train prompt frameworks, and guide teams in how to cocreate with AI. Think creative *conductor*, not creative *director*.

- **You must set the guardrails**—on bias, brand voice, privacy, and consumer trust. Develop AI principles, define red lines, and embed human oversight. Reputation moves faster than results. AI won't just change your tools—it will disrupt workflows, roles, and mindsets. You need to be a transformation leader. Coach your team. Manage fear. Evangelize wins. Reward experimentation. AI strategy is 30 percent tech and 70 percent culture shift.

Chapter 5
Finding, Keeping, and Nurturing
Top Marketing Talent

Marketing has never been more important—or more misunderstood. Once the playground of bold ideas and brand jingles, the field is now a battleground of data, martech, and performance metrics. Somewhere between the spreadsheets and the storytelling, the industry's greatest competitive advantage has emerged: talent. As Coca-Cola's Shakir Moin says, "World-class people build world-class brands."

Finding the right marketing talent today is like finding truffles in a forest—rare, valuable, and often hiding where you least expect it. This is no longer just about creative flair or media muscle. The modern marketer needs to be as comfortable in a pivot table as in a brainstorm. Today's job descriptions read like tech résumés: growth analyst, CRM architect, marketing technologist. These aren't just buzzwords—they're the backbone of how brands grow.

But here's the real challenge: keeping that talent. The industry is facing what the World Federation of Advertisers called its "worst-ever crisis" when it comes to talent. Overworked. Undertrained. And in many cases, undervalued. While demand grows—Statista projects a 7 percent increase in US marketing manager roles by 2032—so does disillusionment: 68 percent of marketers believe it's harder to land a job in the industry now than five years ago. That's not just a stat—it's a signal.

At R3, we've seen firsthand what happens when marketing is treated like a function, not a force. And too many marketers, frankly, outsource the hard parts—strategy, creativity, innovation. But you can't outsource your way to goosebumps.

This chapter is about reversing that trend. It's a call to build from the inside out. To find the rebels, the round pegs, the ones who still believe marketing can change the world—and then give them the tools, the culture, and the mission to actually do it.

Because talent isn't your HR problem. It's your growth strategy.

Smart Team Design

Smart team design isn't just an HR exercise—it's a strategic imperative. In marketing, where the pace of change is relentless and the tools shift by the quarter, how you assemble your team can be the difference between chaos and clarity. Great marketing doesn't happen by accident. It happens when the right people are connected to the right problems, in the right structure.

"I'm not a micromanager," says Lenovo's Emily Ketchen. "I will give my teams all of the openness to go run their own businesses, but I want people who are smarter than me and better than me in my organization, because it pushes all of us. If you're the smartest person in the room . . . you hired wrong."

Leading models like T-shaped talent (depth in one area, breadth across others) and the squad/tribe frameworks from agile tech teams are now being borrowed by modern leaders. These approaches foster collaboration, reduce handoffs, and build resilience.

At R3, we've seen smart team design unlock dormant potential. A centralized strategy team. Embedded data partners. Creative pods linked directly to category heads. It's less about org charts and more about orchestration.

Think of Netflix's pivot: moving from regional silos to content-centric teams. That wasn't cosmetic—it was catalytic. It brought marketers closer to creators, tightened feedback loops, and aligned output with audience demand. In a world where speed and relevance matter more than perfection, smart team design creates flow.

"L'Oréal's growth is fueled by our people," says Asmita Dubey. "We're rewriting the rules of marketing, constantly evolving job descriptions to reflect the ever-changing digital landscape, from advocacy and influence to AI-powered media. We're not just recruiting talent; we're cultivating it. Our immersive onboarding programs ensure new hires embrace L'Oréal's dynamic culture and contribute meaningfully from day one."

The Unique Needs of the Marketing Organization

Hiring for marketing isn't like hiring for finance or ops—it demands a different lens. Too often, hiring managers rely on outdated playbooks, chasing big-brand résumés or familiar titles without understanding what actually drives marketing performance today.

In a world where creativity, data, and agility must coexist, the stakes are high—and the mistakes are costly.

Marketing roles require hybrid skill sets, emotional intelligence, and a tolerance for ambiguity. Miss that, and you don't just get the wrong hire—you slow down the entire team.

Here's where most hiring managers go wrong and what makes marketing talent uniquely different:

* **Hiring for titles, not talent models:** They look for "brand managers" or "media leads" instead of identifying the shape of talent needed—T-shaped, Pi-shaped, or specialist.

  "We've become very disciplined in talent development," says Coca-Cola's Shakir Moin. *"We are more diligent in how we add talent, checking fit and always asking if there's a better way to address the capability gap."*

- **Prioritizing pedigree over potential:** Too much weight is put on big-brand experience and not enough on adaptability, collaboration, or curiosity—critical traits in fast-evolving marketing teams.

- **Overlooking cross-functional fluency:** Marketing doesn't live in a silo. Yet many hires struggle to collaborate with product, tech, or data teams because that wasn't prioritized in the brief.

  "The root of everything is insights," says Cheryl Guerin of Mastercard. "On the front end, our insight teams find those interesting nuggets that create differentiation from what everybody else is looking at, and those motivations that enable us to connect emotionally with consumers or businesses enable us to stand out and break through. On the back end, they help us optimize and measure impact that enables us to keep investing."

  "Marketing Inside is about bringing the future and the consumer into other departments—and not just the friendly ones but also the finance teams, for example, so that they realize the true business value of the consumer connection," says Ed Bell of Cathay Pacific.

- **Misjudging creative confidence:** They hire safe operators instead of creative problem solvers who can push thinking, challenge briefs, and inspire teams.

- **Failing to test for digital fluency:** Digital first isn't a department—it's the default. Hiring managers still assume that digital skills equal "social media knowledge," missing depth in analytics, performance, and automation.

  "We're nurturing a new breed of marketer that can flex a dual muscle," says L'Oréal's Dubey. "These individuals

blend artistry and data science to engineer consumer engagement in the digital age."

Marketing organizations operate on a unique blend of logic and magic—requiring hybrid skill sets that traditional hiring often overlooks. Success in marketing depends on more than technical ability; it demands strategic storytelling, emotional intelligence, and the agility to thrive amid ambiguity and rapid change. Marketers must connect data with culture, collaborate across product and tech, and create relevance in real time. Yet many hiring managers miss these traits, focusing instead on static résumés or narrow expertise. The best marketers aren't defined by function—they're defined by how they think, connect, and move. That's what marketing orgs truly need.

"You have to paint a clear vision of where you're going. And, I mean, three to five years out, what do you want to become?" says Toyota's Mike Tripp. "Then you have to recruit, hire and promote leaders that are going to not only subscribe to that vision, but also can motivate, inspire, and communicate. I believe culture, communication, and inspiration are really the keys to leading a team. You also need to bring humility and fun to the mix. And then you execute by trusting and supporting each other at all levels."

Finding: The Right Type of Talent

Recruiters can't just hire for job descriptions—they need to hire for impact, adaptability, and team chemistry. That's where talent models come in. A talent model is a framework that defines the skills, depth, and breadth of expertise needed in a role to build high-performing, adaptable teams. Hiring without a talent model is like building a puzzle without knowing the picture. You risk overlap, blind spots, or hiring a great specialist into the wrong structure.

Here are some common talent models:

- **T-shaped talent:** The vertical bar of the *T* represents deep expertise in one core area—say, media strategy, CRM, content creation, or analytics. The horizontal bar reflects broad knowledge across other disciplines, allowing the individual to collaborate effectively, understand context, and adapt across teams.

- **I-shaped talent**: Deep expertise in one area with little crossover capability. Great for specialists but often a struggle in collaborative or agile environments.

- **Pi (π)-shaped talent:** Deep expertise in two areas (e.g., analytics and storytelling) and broad understanding across disciplines. This model is ideal for modern marketing leaders—think a growth marketer who also excels in data science and brand strategy.

- **M-shaped talent:** Depth in multiple areas—often seen in senior executives or polymaths. More rare but highly valuable. These people can lead transformation across silos.

- **Comb-shaped talent:** Found in agencies or consulting—breadth in several areas with moderate depth in each. Think generalists who can plug into many projects with agility.

The T-shaped talent model is one of the most widely used frameworks in modern marketing organizations—and for good reason. It balances deep expertise with broad collaboration, which is exactly what today's fast-moving, cross-functional teams demand. In marketing, a T-shaped talent might be a brand strategist who can write a killer brief (deep skill) but also understands martech, paid social, and customer experience design (broad fluency). These are the bridge builders. The ones who move fastest inside modern organizations.

In the age of AI and cross-functional workflows, T- and Pi-shaped models are thriving. Because the future belongs to those who go deep and connect wide.

Finding: The Right Roles to Hire

Over the past two years, marketing roles have undergone a seismic shift—fueled by AI, automation, and the unrelenting demand for personalization at scale. The classic titles of brand manager and media buyer haven't disappeared, but they've been joined—and in some cases replaced—by a new breed of hybrid marketers.

We've seen the rise of titles like the following:

- *Marketing technologist*—bridging the gap between martech stacks and strategy
- *Growth analyst*—laser focused on performance data, customer acquisition, and funnel optimization
- *Content strategist*—not just writing copy but architecting content ecosystems powered by SEO, social signals, and storytelling
- *CRM and life cycle manager*—owning customer journeys end to end, with precision timing and personalization
- *Prompt engineer*—a post-GPT role, designing AI interactions that generate high-quality creative and data outputs

Capabilities have expanded beyond communications. Today's marketers need fluency in data interpretation, platform integration, agile ways of working, and experience design. The line between product, tech, and marketing has blurred—and in smart organizations, it's been erased.

This evolution isn't just about titles—it's about talent that can think holistically, move cross-functionally, and deliver with urgency. The marketers leading growth today are half strategist, half scientist, and 100 percent collaborative.

Marketers can't afford to build teams based on nostalgia. To compete today, they need to audit talent the way they audit spend—with clarity, urgency, and alignment to business outcomes.

Step One: Start with the Customer Journey

Every hiring decision should ladder up to delivering a better experience. Map the journey from awareness to advocacy, and ask, "Where are we strong? Where are we slow? Where are we invisible?" If you're great at brand storytelling but weak in CRM or analytics, the gaps become clear.

Step Two: Build Around Growth, Not Legacy

Too many organizations protect roles that no longer deliver impact. If a function exists just because "we've always done it that way," it's a candidate for sunset. Ask, "Is this role still driving growth? Is it future proofed against automation or AI?"

"Surround yourself with a diverse team," says Eric Lempel of Sony Interactive Entertainment. "By that, I mean you shouldn't have only creative marketers or just data-driven marketers. Having a good mix ensures all voices are heard, so nothing gets overlooked. It needs to be a balanced mix. Given the size of the group and the diverse portfolio, I like to combine industry expertise with classically trained marketing professionals."

Step Three: Don't Just Hire—Retool

Many roles don't need to go—they need to evolve. Your brand manager might need to become a platform strategist. Your media buyer might need to understand API integrations and data clean rooms. Upskilling should be a default, not a fallback.

L'Oréal: Reinventing Marketing Roles for the Digital Age

When L'Oréal declared it wanted to be the world's number one beauty tech company, it didn't start with a new ad—it started with a new org chart.

"Marketing is in perpetual transformation," says Chief Digital and Marketing Officer Asmita Dubey. "We've moved from digital-first to data-powered, experience-driven, and purpose-led. The future demands equipping our teams with both creative brilliance and technological mastery. We call this Augmented Marketing."

For decades, L'Oréal had operated like most global consumer brands: traditional brand managers overseeing campaigns, regional teams adapting global assets, and media planners optimizing buys across markets. But by 2021, it was clear the old playbook wasn't built for a world of TikTok influencers, real-time commerce, and AI-driven personalization.

L'Oréal introduced a new class of hybrid roles:

- *Chief digital officers* were embedded in business units—not as support but as coleaders of growth.
- *Social listening analysts and data scientists* were brought in-house to work alongside creative teams.
- *Content factory leads* emerged—tasked with producing modular, scalable assets tailored for platform, region, and moment.
- Traditional "media managers" were upskilled into *digital investment specialists*, fluent in algorithmic buying and data compliance.

But the biggest shift? Marketing became a tech competency. L'Oréal partnered with Salesforce, Google, and Meta—not just for media but for talent development. Over eighty-five thousand employees received digital upskilling, from AI basics to e-commerce optimization. "The math and the magic must coexist," says Dubey. "Data empowers creativity, allowing us to achieve both speed and scale—essential for a global beauty leader like L'Oréal. You have to marry the creativity and technology. And once you marry it, it can be a very potent combination."

The result? L'Oréal doubled its e-commerce share in under two years and now generates over 25 percent of global revenue online.

This wasn't just new roles. It was a new mindset. Marketing wasn't the megaphone—it was the engine room. And by redesigning teams around agility, platforms, and data, L'Oréal made beauty not just desirable—but downloadable.

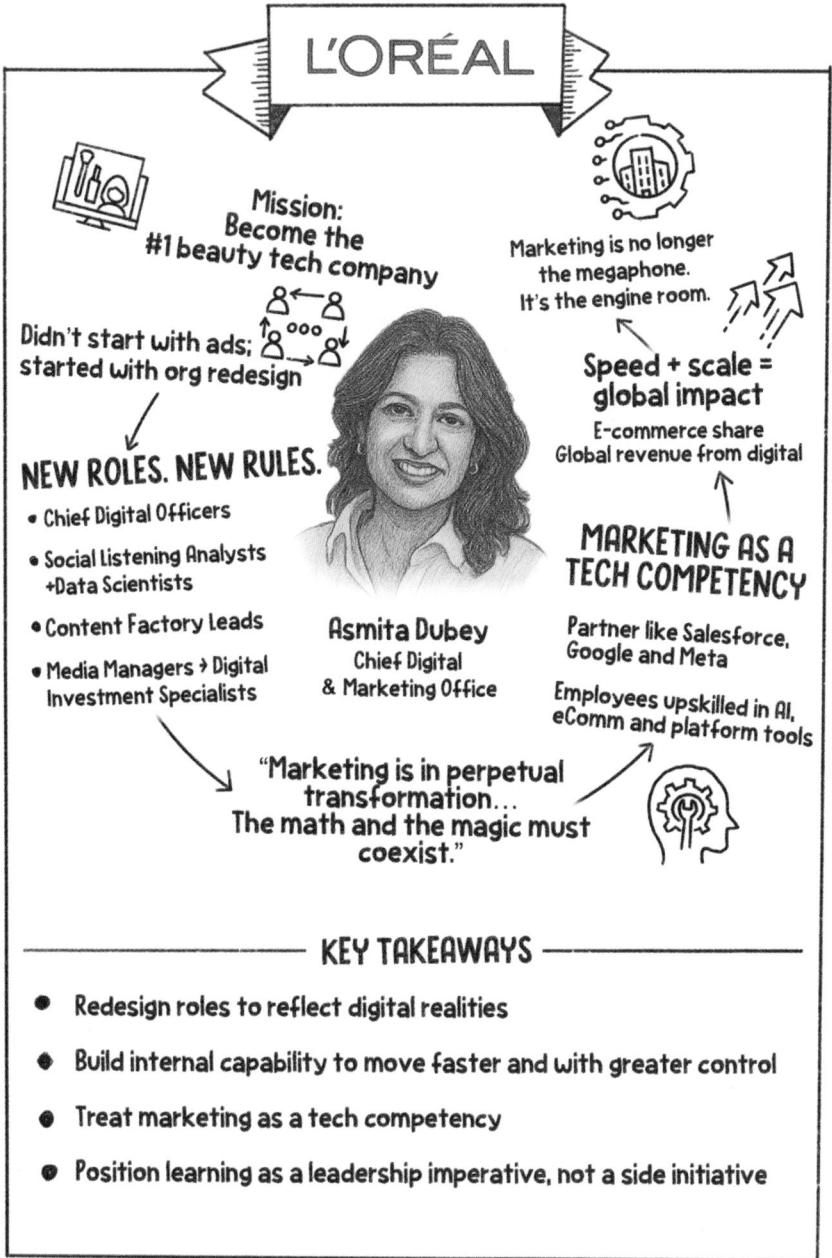

L'ORÉAL

Mission: Become the #1 beauty tech company

Marketing is no longer the megaphone. It's the engine room.

Didn't start with ads; started with org redesign

Speed + scale = global impact
E-commerce share
Global revenue from digital

NEW ROLES. NEW RULES.

- Chief Digital Officers
- Social Listening Analysts +Data Scientists
- Content Factory Leads
- Media Managers → Digital Investment Specialists

Asmita Dubey
Chief Digital
& Marketing Office

MARKETING AS A TECH COMPETENCY

Partner like Salesforce, Google and Meta

Employees upskilled in AI, eComm and platform tools

"Marketing is in perpetual transformation… The math and the magic must coexist."

--- **KEY TAKEAWAYS** ---

- Redesign roles to reflect digital realities
- Build internal capability to move faster and with greater control
- Treat marketing as a tech competency
- Position learning as a leadership imperative, not a side initiative

Key takeaways:

- Redesign roles to reflect digital realities, embedding digital fluency into the core of brand building.
- Build internal capability to move faster, with greater control over creative, data, and personalization.
- Treat marketing as a tech competency, train teams in AI, e-commerce, and platform partnerships.
- Position learning as a leadership imperative—not a side initiative.

Keeping: Giving Talent a Reason to Stay

The marketing industry is in the midst of a talent crisis—and the data proves it. Nearly half of global marketing leaders say we're facing the worst talent shortage in history. In the United States, marketer tenure has shrunk to just 2.6 years, with high performers in data and digital fields being aggressively poached. Retention is slipping, and roles in analytics, martech, and e-commerce are the hardest to fill. Meanwhile, 68 percent of marketers feel it's tougher to find a job now than five years ago. The industry is churning—and unless we rethink talent strategy, the best will keep walking out the door.

"We are focused on cutting-edge, passion and purpose-led innovation, which has become a magnet for talent," says Mastercard's Cheryl Guerin. "The work we do around the world is a source of pride for our employees. That not only creates talent pull and retention internally, but it also attracts talent externally. From our longtime cause-related platform with Stand Up to Cancer, to our True Name and Touch card features, or our Mastercard Artist Accelerator program, the work we do connects emotionally with cardholders and our employees."

Keeping high-performing marketing talent today is harder than ever—and not because they're job hoppers. It's because the job, for many, has stopped delivering meaning, momentum, or mastery.

"Getting great talent comes down to three things. Are people doing exciting work? Are they being trained to do the right things? And do they see themselves growing in that organization?" says Colgate-Palmolive's Mukul Deoras. "The culture of the organization ultimately defines whether you are driving great work or driving exciting work or you're not driving good work at all."

Those who manage in-house teams are focused with an even greater imperative. In-house teams don't have the luxury of a deep bench across global offices. Every hire matters. When a high performer leaves, it's not just a gap—it's a slowdown in speed, creativity, and institutional knowledge. The cost isn't just in recruitment—it's in lost momentum. Great in-house teams thrive on trust, proximity, and shared context. When talent sticks, they build deep brand fluency, move faster, and anticipate needs before they're briefed. They become brand stewards, not just service providers.

What Makes Marketing Talent Leave

Marketing has become one of the toughest industries in which to retain talent—not because marketers aren't committed but because the system around them isn't built to keep up.

First, there's burnout. Marketing today is 24-7, multiplatform, and under constant scrutiny. Between real-time content demands, evolving martech stacks, and shrinking budgets, many marketers feel like they're sprinting a marathon. According to a recent LinkedIn Workforce Report, average tenure in marketing has dropped to just 2.6 years—a clear signal that people are burning out and opting out.

Second, career stagnation is real. The industry moves fast, but internal career paths often don't. A *Marketing Week* Career and Salary Survey found that 57 percent of marketers felt their company offered no clear growth path. In a talent market driven by learning and momentum, that's a red flag.

"There has been a constant push in learning multiple disciplines, pushing people to the edge of their comfort zone, and making them understand why we must learn so much more," says Coca-Cola's Shakir Moin. "For example, we brought in neuroscience in a big way to decode messaging and advertising and human behavior. For most of our marketers, it was a new capability."

Third, there's a growing skills mismatch. The World Federation of Advertisers reported that nearly half of global advertisers believe marketing is facing its "worst-ever talent crisis," particularly in data, e-commerce, and tech-driven roles. Companies want hybrid marketers but rarely invest in upskilling the talent they already have.

Finally, marketers want purpose. When creativity is sidelined and marketing is treated as execution, not strategy—people leave. Not for better pay but for more meaningful impact. Retention isn't just about perks. It's about purpose, progression, and being seen.

"Our values are Caring, Inclusive, and Courageous," says Colgate-Palmolive's Mukul Deoras. "Caring and Inclusive, you would have expected, but Courageous? The core—and the more important—facet of courage is the courage of conviction. Having a belief. Courage to have a point of view. Having the psychological comfort within the organization to be someone who expresses an opinion, and therefore, create that courageous culture where people are free to talk to each other, contribute to each other, and have an independent point of view."

"I think that the best way to motivate and to inspire is to lead by example," says Lenovo's Emily Ketchen. "Your ability to be curious, your ability to take risks, your ability to define and crystallize a vision—all this matters. No one follows a leader who isn't walking the walk."

Let's Talk About Pay

Marketing salaries have shifted—but not always in ways that keep top talent anchored. In some roles, compensation has grown. In others, it's flatlined, even as expectations have doubled. The result? A widening tension between what marketers are asked to deliver and how they're rewarded.

According to a recent *Marketing Week* Career and Salary Survey, average marketing salaries in the United Kingdom rose by just 2.8 percent, well below inflation—meaning many marketers experienced a pay cut in real terms. In the United States, LinkedIn's Workforce Report shows higher wage growth in performance and digital roles (e.g., SEO, CRM, media buying) but stagnant growth in traditional brand roles. Data and martech specialists have seen up to 6 to 9 percent increases, while generalists often stayed flat.

The real challenge isn't just base pay—it's perceived value. Marketers tasked with mastering AI, driving personalization at scale, and optimizing ROI across dozens of platforms are asking, "Am I being paid for the job I was hired for . . . or the ten new ones added since?"

Salary gaps also play into retention. Top performers in high-demand roles are being aggressively poached—with counteroffers becoming the norm. Meanwhile, many in-house teams struggle to match the speed (and cash) of tech and agency offers.

If you want to keep the best, it's not just about perks or titles. It's about aligning pay with impact—and recognizing that when the job changes, the reward must too. Otherwise, the talent you've trained and trusted will leave—and take your momentum with them.

Kraft Heinz: The Kitchen

Kraft Heinz's in-house agency, The Kitchen, has rapidly expanded since its inception, growing from ten to over one hundred employees within a few years. This growth reflects Kraft Heinz's commitment to attracting and retaining top-tier creative talent. Several strategies have been pivotal in this endeavor:

- The Kitchen offers its team the opportunity to produce "acts, not ads," focusing on creating culturally resonant work that engages audiences meaningfully. This approach appeals to creatives seeking to make a tangible impact.
- The agency fosters a culture where egos are set aside and collaboration is prioritized. This democratic approach to creativity ensures that all team members feel valued and are encouraged to contribute their unique perspectives.

- Kraft Heinz invests in its employees' development, providing avenues for skill enhancement and career progression. This commitment to growth attracts ambitious professionals eager to advance in their careers.
- Working within The Kitchen allows creatives to engage directly with Kraft Heinz's portfolio of well-known brands. This direct involvement offers a unique opportunity to shape brand narratives and execute innovative campaigns.

Key takeaways:

- Invest in in-housing for faster content production, real-time campaign iteration, and better alignment with brand tone.
- Rather than hiring more, teach marketers how to operate like creators, data analysts, and media optimizers.
- Embed cultural relevance and rapid-response content into your marketing DNA.
- Train marketers to interpret and act on performance data.

Attracting and Retaining Talent

Being a real leader today is a balancing act on a high wire—strategic one minute, surgical the next. You're expected to be the external face of the brand, the internal voice of the customer, and the connective tissue between creative, commercial, and C-suite priorities. You've got to think about market share, campaign impact, tech stacks, and shareholder expectations. But here's what often gets missed: Your internal team is watching how you lead just as closely as your board is watching what you deliver.

If the talent doesn't believe in the mission, if they're not growing, if they don't feel seen—you don't have a marketing team. You have attrition in slow motion.

"We are in a growth category, one that people are generally very interested

in," says Glanbia's Colin Westcott-Pitt. "That helps with conversations, and we're able to paint what we hope is a fairly inspirational picture about our brands."

Great heads understand that their job isn't just to sell the brand to consumers—it's to sell the organization to current and future talent. That starts inside. It means being visible in stand-ups, asking better questions in creative reviews, and making sure "brand purpose" doesn't die in a slide but lives in the culture. It means giving marketers room to think, to test, to fail, and to find their voice.

Too many get caught in the external optics—driving growth, managing media spend, presenting to the board. That's important. But the real power lies in the team behind you. Are they staying? Are they learning? Would they follow you into a new role tomorrow?

Talent doesn't leave because of workload. They leave because of a lack of momentum, a lack of recognition, or a lack of belief. And that belief—more than budgets, more than strategy decks—is what you must protect. Leadership in marketing today isn't about having all the answers. It's about setting the conditions for others to find them.

Here's how you can lead from the inside out:

- **Set clarity, not just vision:** Teams don't need more mantras—they need direction. Define what success looks like *this quarter*, not just "someday." Align people to business outcomes, not vague brand goals.
- **Be present:** The best don't disappear behind strategy decks. They show up—to creative reviews, team stand-ups, postcampaign retros. Presence signals importance. It builds trust.
- **Champion capability:** Don't wait for HR to upskill your team. Invest in training, cross-functional exposure, and mentorship. The smartest make learning part of the culture—not just learning and development line item.
- **Protect the thinkers:** Great ideas need space. Shield your team from bureaucracy and performative process. Give them room to fail fast and

permission to build boldly.

- **Share credit and take accountability:** When campaigns win, make heroes of your team. When results dip, own it. That balance builds loyalty like nothing else.

Nurturing: Elevating Talent

Two years ago, upskilling in marketing meant sending someone to a branding workshop or brushing up on the latest media metrics. Today, it means something entirely different. It means teaching your team to think like analysts, behave like technologists, and move like entrepreneurs.

"We created our own marketing education and centralized it in a digital hub," says Toyota's Mike Tripp. "We didn't leave it to HR or other corporate training groups. We've created and pulled together internal, agency, and external content and prescribed curriculum by role—like you would if you were going to college based on your job level—and we tie completion to personal development plans and ultimately performance reviews."

Modern marketing upskilling is about building hybrid humans—creatives who can read dashboards, media planners who understand AI prompts, brand leads who can cocreate with product and tech. It's not about nice-to-have training sessions. It's about survival.

The challenges are real. The pace of change is brutal—new platforms, tools, and algorithms arrive faster than most teams can adapt. Marketers are already stretched thin, so asking them to "learn more" often feels like one more weight on the barbell. Worse still, many companies roll out one-size-fits-all training programs that miss the point—great-performance media leads don't need storytelling basics. And if leadership isn't walking the talk, even the best programs fall flat.

But the upside? It's huge.

Companies that invest in real, role-relevant upskilling see talent stay longer, work smarter, and contribute deeper. Internal teams become more autonomous—less dependent on agencies, more in control of their narrative.

Speed improves. So does innovation.

We've seen this firsthand. Marketers who go through thoughtful upskilling programs don't just learn—they start leading. They spot opportunities others miss. They drive growth from the inside out. Upskilling today isn't about turning marketers into coders. It's about giving them the confidence and tools to thrive in a marketing world that's never been more technical, more measurable, or more exciting.

Designing Upskilling Programs

Training in marketing isn't like training in other functions. You're not teaching people to follow a process—you're teaching them to stay ahead of it. Marketing teams operate at the speed of culture, tech, and consumer expectation. That means yesterday's playbook won't win tomorrow's brief.

"One of the things that we did was we started an internal training and education series called the Spark Series, which is all about bringing in industry luminaries and having real conversations about the importance of marketing, AI, and more. Sometimes all it takes is one spark to ignite a new way of thinking," says Lenovo's Emily Ketchen.

What makes capability building in marketing unique is the constant need to bridge creativity and commercial thinking. One day it's storytelling; the next, it's first-party data strategy or prompt engineering. That's why training must be real time, role relevant, and ruthlessly practical. The best programs don't just teach—they transform how people show up at work the next day.

At R3, we've seen too many companies invest in content libraries, only to find that no one uses them. Why? Because marketing talent doesn't need theory—they need tools they can apply now. Capability programs must be built for action, not attendance.

"Curiosity is a big factor that we value and the sign of a naturally intuitive marketer," says Glanbia's Colin Westcott-Pitt. "We also put a lot of emphasis on understanding of product. We have a product education program called the sports nutrition school with over 150,000 employee and trade graduates globally over the last 15 years."

The best marketing organizations treat training not as a checkbox but as a competitive edge. Because in a world where every marketer is expected to deliver ROI and relevance, the only way to win is to keep learning faster than the world changes.

Here are some considerations for your next training program:

- **Start with roles, not buzzwords:** AI impacts different roles differently. A media planner needs to understand algorithmic bidding and attribution modeling. A creative needs to master generative tools and modular content design. Tailor training to role-specific realities—not just hype.

- **Teach application, not theory:** Marketers don't need to become data scientists—but they do need to understand how AI shapes targeting, creative iteration, and customer journeys. Focus on practical skills: building smarter briefs, evaluating AI-generated assets, interpreting machine-led insights.

- **Blend human and machine capabilities:** AI can automate execution, but humans still lead insight, intuition, and imagination. Upskilling should emphasize how to collaborate with AI—when to trust it, when to override it, and how to enhance it with human judgment.

- **Prioritize ethical literacy:** As AI scales, so do risks—bias, misinformation, and creative misuse. Marketers need frameworks for responsible AI use. Not just "Can we use this model?" but "Should we?"

- **Embed continuous learning:** AI is evolving daily. So must your upskilling program. Move from one-off trainings to a culture of experimentation: labs, live demos, peer-sharing sessions, cross-functional projects.

- **Align with business goals:** Upskilling in AI shouldn't be a tech showcase—it should drive impact. Whether that's faster go-to-market, smarter segmentation, or higher ROI, make the connection clear.

A Word About Talent in the Age of AI

The threat of AI to marketing talent isn't robots replacing people—it's people becoming irrelevant because they didn't evolve.

AI is already transforming how campaigns are planned, content is created, and performance is optimized. Tools can now write copy, generate visuals, predict customer behavior, and even automate media buys—and do it faster, cheaper, and often more accurately than humans. The risk isn't that marketers will be replaced entirely. It's that marketers who don't adapt will be left behind.

The biggest threats include the following:

- **Commoditization of skills:** Entry-level tasks—copywriting, A/B testing, basic analytics—are now automated. Talent that doesn't move beyond these functions risks being seen as expendable.

- **Shrinking creative ownership:** As generative AI enters the creative stack, marketers may lose control over the ideation process unless they lead its use. If AI drives the ideas, what's left for the human?

- **Performance pressure:** AI brings hypermeasurement—and with it, higher expectations. Marketers who can't link creativity to ROI, or strategy to data, may be sidelined.

- **Organizational shift:** AI favors flatter, faster, cross-functional teams. Rigid hierarchies and legacy roles may be phased out in favor of agile hybrids who can build, interpret, and act on AI outputs.

When AI entered the marketing mainstream, many leaders panicked. Tools that could write copy, build media plans, even design logos—overnight, it felt like the machines were coming for the work we used to value most. But here's the truth: The threat isn't AI. It's how we treat our people in response to it.

At R3, we've seen it too often—leaders freeze hiring, cut training budgets, and quietly phase out roles without ever explaining why. That's not strategy. That's fear.

The smartest, though? They do the opposite. They treat AI not as a threat but as a turning point—and they treat their teams like growth partners, not line items.

They start with honesty: "Yes, things are changing. But we're going to change with them." Then they act. They reframe roles—turning copywriters into creative conductors of AI-generated content. They train media managers to become interpreters of machine learning. They put real money into upskilling, not just tools.

And most importantly, they create space for curiosity. They encourage experiments. They admit they don't have all the answers. Because the best ideas won't come from the tech—they'll come from the humans who know how to use it with taste, timing, and empathy.

That's how you lead through disruption.

Chapter 6
Marketing Outside:
Working with Agencies

I've always believed that the relationship between marketers and their agencies is akin to a dance—sometimes it's a graceful waltz, other times a chaotic tango. No one outside the industry truly understands the full role agencies play in the marketing process because few companies outsource other functions to the same extent.

Making the right long-term selection is a little like finding a marriage partner. And often historically, that's where we come in—like a priest at a wedding.

And like all dynamic relationships, the interplay between brands and their agencies has evolved with time. The healthiest brand-agency "relationships" today balance independence with collaboration, excitement with stability, and clear commitments with the freedom to grow.

- **From long-term marriage to flexible dating:** Twenty years ago, brands and agencies often "married" under one long-term agency of record contract—akin to a traditional, monogamous marriage. Today, many brands have felt the itch for variety. They're "dating" multiple specialist partners on short-term, project-by-project arrangements, swapping pod-based teams like trying new dinner spots, and keeping the relationship exciting and agile.

- **Moving in together—and sometimes apart:** Just as some couples choose to merge households to save rent and align schedules, two-thirds of brands have built in-house agencies—bringing creative and media "chores" under their own roof. This gives them quicker decision-making and a clearer understanding of day-to-day life. But, like partners who need their own space, brands still enlist external experts for the occasional big campaign "road trip."

- **Blended families of services:** In modern blended families, stepsiblings learn to share living space and resources just as WPP, Publicis, and Omnicom have fused creative, data, and tech into one integrated "household." Brands enjoy shared infrastructure and real-time insight—much like a large family sharing a communal calendar—but sometimes struggle with who's responsible for which chore.

- **Growing independence and self-care:** Advances in AI are like one partner picking up a new solo hobby—suddenly brands can design ads, optimize bids, and segment audiences themselves, without leaning on the other person. Agencies feel the pressure to reinvent their roles, just like a partner learning new skills to stay relevant and valued in the relationship.

- **"Prenups" and performance-based vows:** Finally, couples today often draft prenuptial agreements outlining what happens if things don't go as planned. Similarly, more brand-agency contracts now tie fees directly to outcomes: sales lifts, acquisition costs, or brand-health metrics. Both sides know exactly what they're promising—and what they'll celebrate—before they say "I do."

Getting the relationship right matters because they change the course of brand history. Great brand-agency relationships can inspire, create culture, and bring people together. Across boardrooms and brainstorms, across creative pitches and procurement calls, the push and pull between brand and agency has shaped some of the greatest marketing achievements in modern business—from Apple's "Think Different," Coca-Cola's "I'd Like to Teach the World to Sing," and Nike's "Just Do It"—these landmark ideas have transformed brands and outcomes.

"The role of agencies is to be provocateurs and champions of the brands in partnership with us, with a finger on the pulse of the zeitgeist, originators of engaging brand building ideas," says Haleon's Tamara Rogers. "Agencies do a fantastic job of reminding us that we might be up against more interesting things in the world of the consumer, who doesn't think all day every day about our brands like we do, push us out of our comfort zone, to be bold as we seek cut-through and branded memorability. They play a really important role in provoking us to think differently, and better, around what we're doing and how we're doing it and where we go."

In the early days, when the likes of David Ogilvy and Bill Bernbach were reshaping how brands talked to consumers, the agency was often treated like an external brain—the place where ideas were born, ads were made, and campaigns were launched. But as the decades rolled on, things shifted. Marketing grew more complex, more fragmented, more data driven. Agencies multiplied. Holding companies consolidated. Technology firms joined the fray. And suddenly, the once-clear lines between client and partner began to blur.

To understand the role of agencies in how marketing operates inside, we need to look outward—to the people, platforms, and partners that help marketers succeed in the world beyond their walls. It's also about looking at the frictions and the breakthroughs in those relationships. We'll examine the Coca-Cola/WPP relationship in detail, dive into what Publicis Groupe is building, and unpack the strategic consequences of the Omnicom and Interpublic merger. We'll explore agency models and how those models are playing out in the wild. And we'll peer into the future—at how generative AI might be the next great disruptor in marketing's long dance with agencies.

Mastercard and McCann: The Long Road to Priceless

In a world where agency relationships are measured in dog years, Mastercard and McCann are practically ancient. And yet—somehow—timeless. The "Priceless" campaign was born in 1997, but what's made it endure isn't nostalgia. It's reinvention. Together, Mastercard and McCann have treated the idea less like a tagline and more like a platform—stretching from TV to touchpoints, from emotional storytelling to experiential design. And as the brand shifted from plastic to platform, McCann came with it.

What makes this relationship successful? Consistency without complacency. McCann didn't just deliver award-winning creative—it embedded itself in the business.

"One ask stays the same," says Cheryl Guerin, Executive Vice President of Global Brand Strategy and Innovation at Mastercard. "They need to continue to focus on breakthrough creative ideas. What we are looking for from our agencies is creative that has an impact on our brand and business. Now more than ever, they need to have the tech capabilities to enable agile, effective, efficient and measurable impact. The more we can move out some of the tactical work to be more efficient, the more investment we can put against creative ideas."

As Mastercard leaned into experiences, McCann evolved the work beyond advertising. "Priceless Cities." "Priceless Surprises." From sonic branding to nonfungible tokens, the campaign became architecture. It flexed. It followed culture.

What makes it distinct? Trust.

Raja Rajamannar, Mastercard's CMO, is one of the most progressive marketing leaders in the world. He's talked openly about the need to reinvent marketing—and yet, he's stuck with McCann. Why? Because reinvention doesn't mean replacement. It means a shared hunger to push forward, together. The agency was never just a vendor. It became a custodian of a brand idea—and a copilot in its transformation.

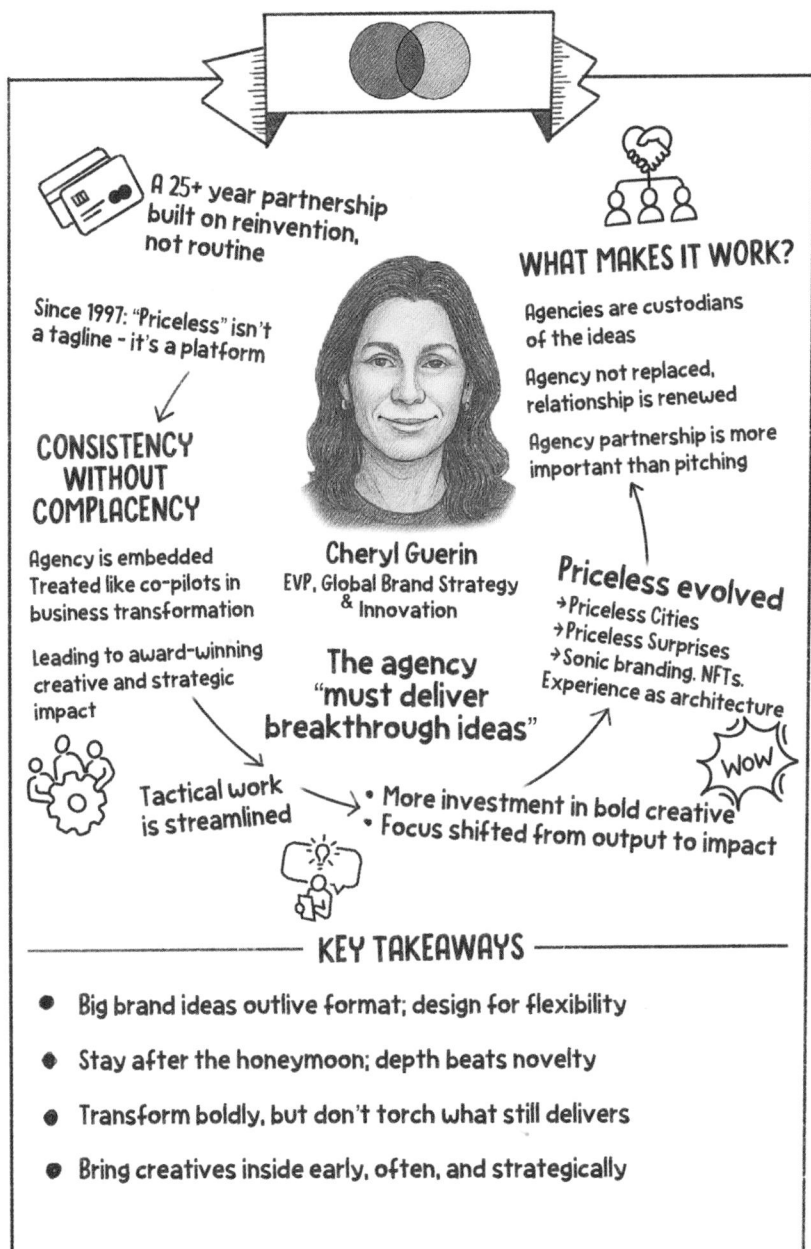

A 25+ year partnership built on reinvention, not routine

Since 1997: "Priceless" isn't a tagline – it's a platform

CONSISTENCY WITHOUT COMPLACENCY

Agency is embedded
Treated like co-pilots in business transformation

Leading to award-winning creative and strategic impact

Tactical work is streamlined

WHAT MAKES IT WORK?

Agencies are custodians of the ideas

Agency not replaced, relationship is renewed

Agency partnership is more important than pitching

Cheryl Guerin
EVP, Global Brand Strategy & Innovation

The agency "must deliver breakthrough ideas"

Priceless evolved
→ Priceless Cities
→ Priceless Surprises
→ Sonic branding. NFTs.
Experience as architecture

WOW

• More investment in bold creative
• Focus shifted from output to impact

--- KEY TAKEAWAYS ---

- Big brand ideas outlive format; design for flexibility
- Stay after the honeymoon; depth beats novelty
- Transform boldly, but don't torch what still delivers
- Bring creatives inside early, often, and strategically

In a category known for shouting features, Mastercard whispered emotion. In a marketing industry obsessed with the new, it showed the power of renewal. In the end, Mastercard and McCann didn't just preserve a great campaign—they proved what's possible when marketers invest in partnership, not just output. When creative isn't outsourced but embedded. When marketing lives inside. Priceless.

Key takeaways:

- Big ideas outlive formats; build brand ideas that are flexible, not fixed.
- The best work often comes after the honeymoon; resist the knee-jerk pitch cycle and invest in deep, strategic alignment.
- Lead transformation without burning down what's working.
- Invite creative partners inside—early, often, and at the highest levels.

Getting the Agency Model Right

An agency model in marketing refers to the way a company structures its relationships and collaborations with external marketing or advertising agencies. It defines who does what, how they're paid, and how success is measured. Ultimately, the best agency model depends on the company's goals, resources, and culture, and over time, major brands have evolved their agency models in response to changing needs, technologies, and expectations.

There are six common types of agency models. These are not theoretical. They're alive, dynamic, and visible in the field. Each has its strengths. Each comes with risk. But understanding them is key to building a model that supports growth, creativity, and control.

- **Multiple best-in-class:** This is the portfolio play. Marketers handpick agencies for their category leadership—digital from one, media from another, social from a third. You get excellence in every vertical, but it comes at the cost of orchestration. Who plays conductor? Often, it's the client. For companies with strong in-house teams and robust marketing ops, this model works well. It's agile, it's talent rich—but it needs internal coordination muscle. This is the most common approach to agency management, but now with the growth of data, influencer, social, generative AI, and other specific agencies, managing them all has become a true labor of love.

- **Lead agency:** Here, one agency—usually the creative agency of record—is tasked with guiding strategy, integrating other partners, and acting as brand steward. The benefits? Clear accountability, consistency in tone and execution, and a point of control. But the risks emerge when the lead lacks influence or isn't empowered. We've seen brilliant lead agencies fail simply because the client didn't enforce alignment across the roster. P&G was the first to try this on several brands a decade ago—even down to the lead agency paying the other partners. Having an active wingman in your integration play makes logical sense—but finding that player for the long term is always a major challenge.

- **Holding company—sister agencies:** A growing number of clients want the benefits of multiple services without the pain of cross-agency friction. So they go to a single holding company and ask for an integrated team. Think Pepsi or AT&T with Omnicom or Unilever with WPP< IPG and OMC. The holding company lines up its best people from different agency brands. They may sit together. They may report separately. But ideally, they operate like a unified team with shared goals and tech. The challenge? Incentives and egos. The agencies still compete on awards, P&L, and prestige.

- **Holding company—custom agency:** This is the model Coca-Cola adopted with WPP—and it's been working well for Apple for over forty years. Instead of stitching together teams from existing agencies, the holding company creates a new entity—OpenX, Team One, Red Fuse, etc. Everyone works on one client. One P&L. One identity. It's highly focused and often delivers rapid results. But it's expensive and resource intensive. Not every brand has the scale to justify it.

- **Free agent:** Think of this as the Hollywood model. No permanent partners. Marketers hire for projects—a pitch here, a stunt there, a quick activation next quarter. It's highly nimble and often used by start-ups or DTC brands. But it lacks continuity and institutional knowledge. And over time, it can wear down internal teams who have to reset the brief every time.

- **One-stop shop:** One agency does everything. Strategy, media, creative, digital, social. It sounds efficient—and it can be. But only if the agency truly has the breadth and depth. It's very common to see this in Japan or Brazil, where media and creative are usually under the same roof. It's also common with smaller marketers who don't want the hassle of multiple agencies. Sometimes this model is a budget decision, not a strategy. And that's where it fails. If you're expecting a Swiss Army knife but get a plastic spork, it's a problem.

In practice, most companies don't live in just one of these models. They evolve. They mix. A brand might use a custom agency globally but a best-in-class stack locally. The trick is knowing your goals—and designing your agency ecosystem to match. Integration isn't about control. It's about connection. And the best marketers are the ones who know how to connect the dots.

The Coca-Cola and WPP Partnership: A New Era of Collaboration

Coca-Cola formed a global brand off the back of McCann Erickson. It seemed that wherever Coke planted its flag, so did McCann. In the olden days of Coca-Cola, people used to get promoted for making advertising—so make it they did. Once the restrictions of the COVID-19 pandemic ended, Coca-Cola found itself with more than four hundred creative agencies, local media relationships with every holding company, and no data spine connecting anything. Quite frankly, it was a mess.

So, in 2021 Coca-Cola announced a strategic global marketing partnership with WPP. On the surface, it looked like a standard holding company win, but underneath it represented a dramatic shift in how one of the world's most recognized brands approached integration. The partnership resulted in the creation of OpenX, a bespoke team within WPP built solely for Coca-Cola—pulling in talent from Ogilvy, VMLY&R, EssenceMediacom, and Hogarth, among others. More than two hundred brands across 190 countries. One agency network. One mission.

Why did Coca-Cola make the leap? It came down to consistency, capability, and culture. Over the years, Coca-Cola's marketing became a patchwork of local executions and varied agency relationships. Some markets leaned heavily into digital; others clung to TV. Creative tone and media weight varied dramatically. WPP offered something most holding companies had only theorized—a fully integrated team that could be as global or as local as Coca-Cola needed.

The promise was grand: one P&L, one point of accountability, and a deep understanding of both the Coca-Cola brand and the nuance required in each region. For WPP, it was the crown jewel of post-Sorrell reinvention. For Coca-Cola, it was a bet that marketing integration could drive creative innovation, faster decision-making, and greater operational efficiency.

But even marriages made in heaven require renegotiation. Recently, Coca-Cola made a notable pivot—moving its North American media business to Publicis Groupe. Sources close to the matter cited a need for agility and a different kind of data capability in that market. This pivot wasn't a rejection of OpenX—it was a recognition that even custom models must flex with business realities.

What can we learn from this? Custom integration is powerful but must be built on adaptability, not rigidity. The Coca-Cola/WPP model is likely to become the blueprint for other global marketers seeking balance between scale and creativity. But it won't be the only model, and it won't be static. As one senior executive put it, "The more integrated we become, the more nimble we must remain."

There's an Agency Model for All Seasons

Just as brands evolve, so too should the way they partner. There is an agency model for every stage of maturity, and knowing which one to adopt (and when) can be the difference between spinning wheels and breaking through.

When you're a **disruptor**—hungry, restless, and eager to grow—your best partners aren't monogamous; they're mercenary. Multiple best-in-class agencies or even a free agent model offers speed, specialism, and experimentation. It's about testing channels, pushing messages, shifting gears in real time. Think full-funnel omnichannel. Think agile. At this stage, your agency model is your playground—and you need partners who can keep up.

As your **brand evolves and matures**, so does your need for emotional resonance and strategic depth. Enter hybrid models, custom agencies, and tight rosters. Here, creativity becomes a shared obsession. You're not just selling; you're building loyalty. Your marketing must create moments that matter—big bets that move minds and hearts. At this point, it's not just about performance—it's about purpose. And your agency model must be built to feel that deeply.

And finally, when you're **playing on the big stage**, leading categories or defining culture, a lead-agency or holding company model often delivers best. Here, cohesion is currency. You're scaling experiences, not just campaigns. Data must flow, talent must flex, and innovation must be constant. It's less about casting and more about choreography.

So yes—there is an agency model for every season of brand life. But the best marketers don't just pick a model and stick with it. They evolve, just like their consumers. They optimize, retool, reimagine. Because the agency model isn't the engine—it's the transmission. And great marketers know exactly when to shift gears.

Colgate and Red Fuse: Built to Fit, Built to Last

In a sea of agency models, Colgate didn't choose off the rack. It tailored its own. Enter Red Fuse—a bespoke, integrated agency created by WPP in 2012 to service Colgate-Palmolive globally. More than just a client-agency relationship, this was a custom-built ecosystem. One brand. One team. One mission.

So, what's made it work?

Proximity. Red Fuse isn't just an external partner—it sits inside Colgate's world. Teams are colocated, embedded across regions, living the rhythms of the business. This closeness eliminates friction. Briefs don't need translation. Alignment doesn't need a calendar.

Integration. Red Fuse houses creative, media, digital, shopper marketing, and strategy under one roof. The left and right brains of the marketing world, fused. The result? Campaigns that think holistically from the start. Media

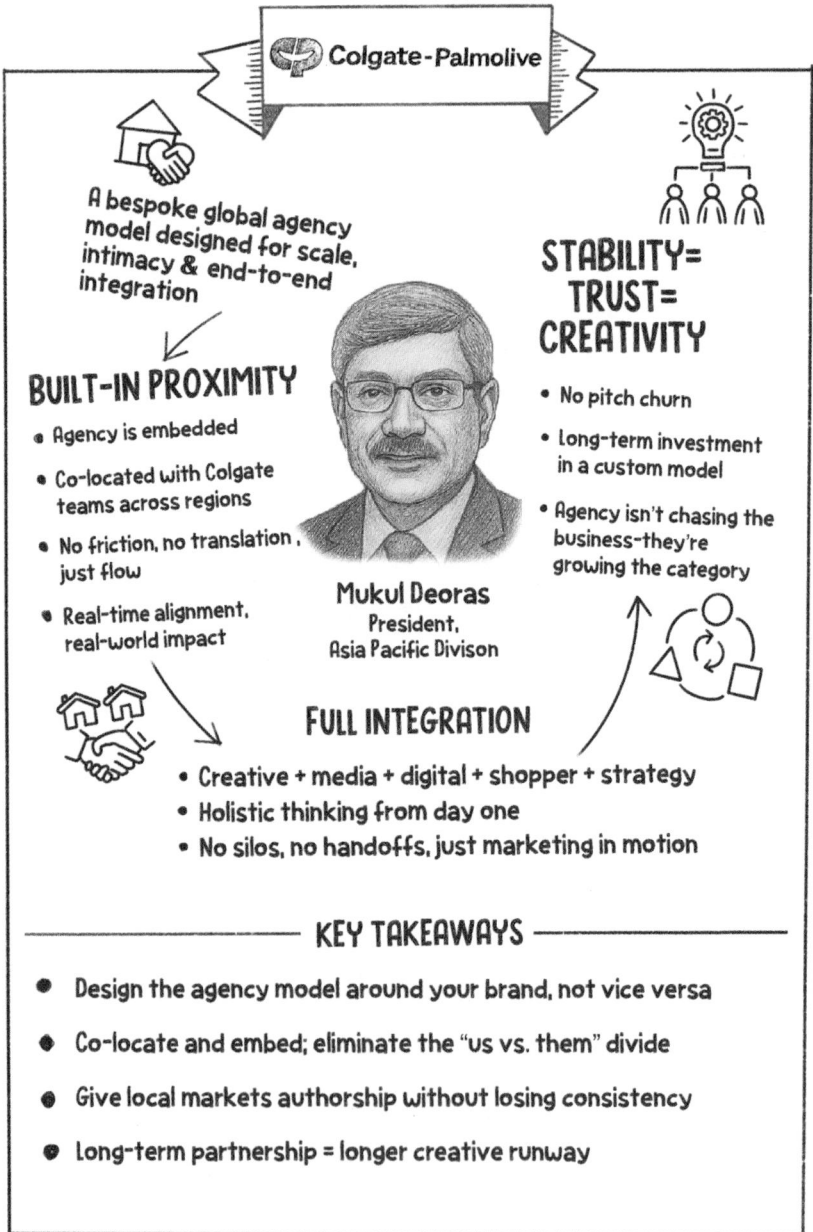

Colgate-Palmolive

A bespoke global agency model designed for scale, intimacy & end-to-end integration

STABILITY= TRUST= CREATIVITY

BUILT-IN PROXIMITY

- Agency is embedded
- Co-located with Colgate teams across regions
- No friction, no translation, just flow
- Real-time alignment, real-world impact

- No pitch churn
- Long-term investment in a custom model
- Agency isn't chasing the business—they're growing the category

Mukul Deoras
President,
Asia Pacific Divison

FULL INTEGRATION

- Creative + media + digital + shopper + strategy
- Holistic thinking from day one
- No silos, no handoffs, just marketing in motion

———— KEY TAKEAWAYS ————

- Design the agency model around your brand, not vice versa
- Co-locate and embed; eliminate the "us vs. them" divide
- Give local markets authorship without losing consistency
- Long-term partnership = longer creative runway

doesn't wait for creative. Strategy isn't a separate step. Execution is end to end.

Global with local teeth. Colgate is a global giant with deep local relevance—from São Paulo to Seoul. Red Fuse has cracked the code on balancing scale with nuance. Local market teams aren't downstream—they're coauthors. It's not just one voice speaking eighty languages—it's eighty voices speaking one brand truth.

What makes it distinct? Colgate didn't chase the latest shiny model. It committed. While other marketers reshuffle their rosters every eighteen months, Colgate invested in building a bespoke solution and stuck with it. That stability has bred trust. And trust has bred creativity. "Marketing is getting so complicated that people get lost in so many things and lose sight of the simplicity of marketing," says Mukul Deoras. Red Fuse isn't trying to win the account—it's trying to win the category. In the end, Red Fuse is more than a name—it's a philosophy. Fuse the right talent. Embed it deep. Think as one. Move as one.

Key takeaways:

- Build the model around your brand, not the other way around.
- Engineer intimacy between teams; great work rarely survives the gaps between "us" and "them."
- Empower local teams without fragmenting the brand.
- See partnership longevity not as comfort but as creative runway.

Toyota, Lexus, and the Saatchi System: A Masterclass in Brand Architecture

In the ever-revolving door of agency reviews and marketing reorgs, Toyota's relationship with Saatchi & Saatchi—and its bespoke Lexus agency, Team One—is a rare and remarkable constant. While others chase novelty, Toyota has quietly built one of the most stable, structured, and strategically sharp client-agency ecosystems in the world.

It starts with clarity.

Toyota isn't one brand—it's a portfolio. The Toyota master brand stands for reliability, innovation, and mass-market leadership. Lexus, on the other hand, is aspiration, craftsmanship, and performance. Most companies would hand that over to two disconnected agencies. Toyota didn't.

It built a system.

Saatchi & Saatchi has been Toyota's North American creative agency since the 1970s—more than four decades of partnership. In an industry where eighteen months is long term, that's a legacy. But what's made it work is reinvention. From the Prius revolution to the hybrid era to the current push into electrification and safety tech, Saatchi hasn't just kept pace—it's helped lead.

For Lexus, Toyota didn't just assign the business to Saatchi. It created Team One—a purpose-built agency with its own culture, talent, and philosophy. Based in El Segundo, Team One wasn't designed to share desks with Camry planners. It was made to sit closer to luxury, lifestyle, and innovation. From launching the first Lexus LS in 1989 to crafting today's global brand tone, Team One has been as much a steward as a spark.

So what makes this structure successful?

- **Segmentation without separation.** Saatchi, Team One, and Toyota's internal teams share values, data, and even talent but never dilute the distinctiveness of the brands they serve. There's alignment without overlap. Collaboration without confusion.
- **Trust and time.** These aren't "keep the lights on" relationships. They're "build the lighthouse" relationships. Mutual investment in each other's

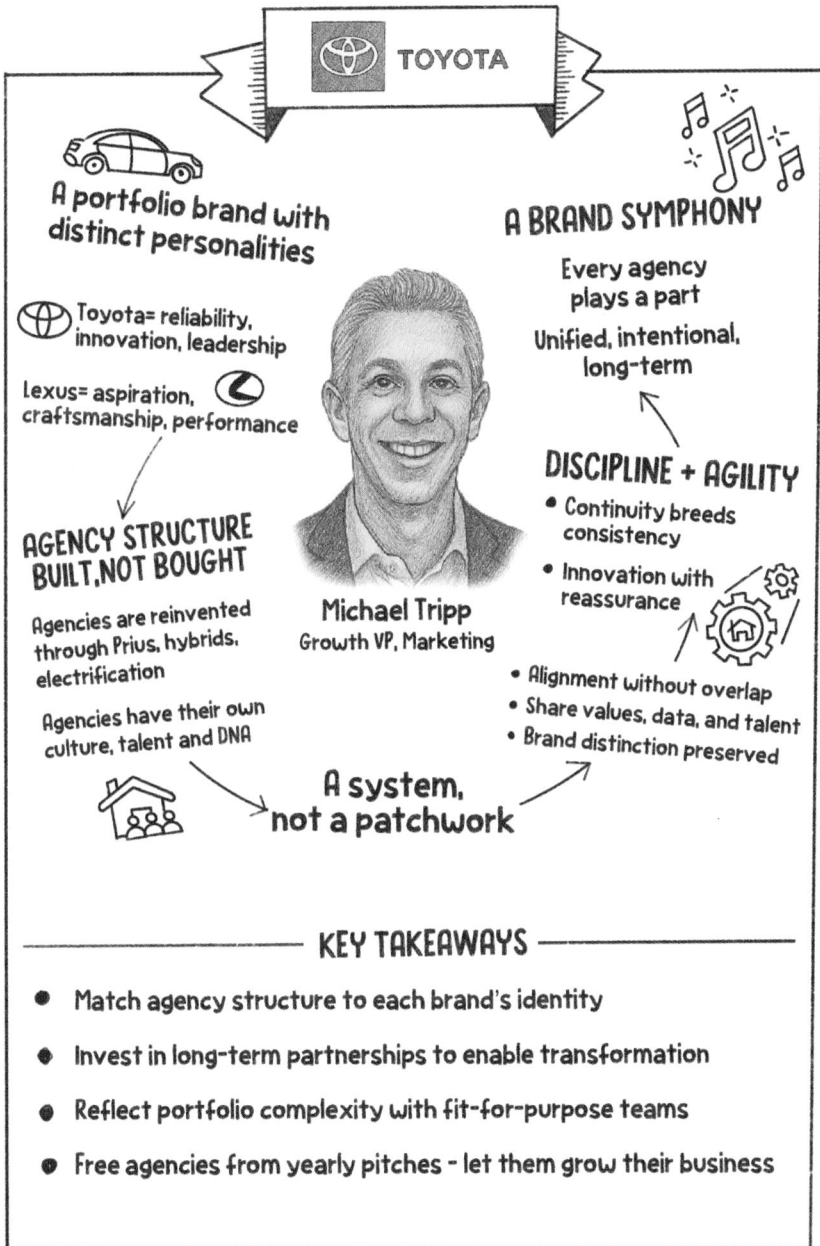

TOYOTA

A portfolio brand with distinct personalities

Toyota= reliability, innovation, leadership

Lexus= aspiration, craftsmanship, performance

AGENCY STRUCTURE BUILT, NOT BOUGHT

Agencies are reinvented through Prius, hybrids, electrification

Agencies have their own culture, talent and DNA

Michael Tripp
Growth VP, Marketing

A system, not a patchwork

A BRAND SYMPHONY

Every agency plays a part

Unified, intentional, long-term

DISCIPLINE + AGILITY
- Continuity breeds consistency
- Innovation with reassurance

- Alignment without overlap
- Share values, data, and talent
- Brand distinction preserved

--- **KEY TAKEAWAYS** ---

- Match agency structure to each brand's identity
- Invest in long-term partnerships to enable transformation
- Reflect portfolio complexity with fit-for-purpose teams
- Free agencies from yearly pitches – let them grow their business

success has led to breakthrough work—like the multicultural "One Team" Super Bowl spots or the Lexus "December to Remember" campaign that's become a seasonal icon.

- **Discipline meets agility.** This isn't legacy for legacy's sake. It's continuity in service of consistency. In a market that demands both innovation and reassurance, Toyota's agency model delivers both.

This isn't just brand stewardship. It's brand symphony. A unified system where every note is intentional, every partner knows their part, and the whole is greater than the horsepower.

Key takeaways:

- Tailor agency structures to the brand's personality.
- See long-term relationships as fertile ground for transformation, not inertia.
- Multiple brands or segments must mirror their portfolio complexity with fit-for-purpose agency teams.
- When your agency doesn't need to "win" the business every year, it can focus on growing it.

Holding Companies: From Partners to Platforms

Once seen as sprawling empires with alphabet soup agency rosters, the giants—Publicis Groupe, IPG, Omnicom, WPP, Dentsu, Havas—have spent the last few years trying to look a lot less like conglomerates and a lot more like partners.

Publicis led the charge with its "Power of One" mantra—bringing data, media, and creative into one operating system. Epsilon and Sapient were no longer sidekicks—they were central characters. They turned their sprawl into structure. Clients didn't want a pitch parade. They wanted answers. Fast.

Omnicom leaned into orchestration. With Omni as its platform, the company made it clear: Integration wasn't a dream—it was code. It placed media and commerce at the heart, layering precision on top of persuasion. Its best talent? Now reachable in real time, across borders, briefs, and brands.

WPP went through an identity refresh of its own. Agencies merged, silos fell, and AKQA and Grey became a new kind of creative force. Under Mark Read, WPP started acting less like a holding company and more like a creative technology company. Experience, commerce, and platforms took the front seat.

IPG doubled down on data with Acxiom. The message? "We know your customer better than you do." But instead of selling spreadsheets, it made data feel human—applying it to ideas, not just impressions.

Dentsu shed its regional skin and focused on becoming a global, integrated powerhouse. The Japanese roots now stretch across strategy, CXM, media, and innovation. Clarity became the currency.

And **Havas**? It bet on "meaningful brands." A smaller player with a sharper message: In a world drowning in noise, meaning matters.

For marketers, this shift in the holding companies is a playbook rewrite and proposes the challenge of which way to align themselves as they look for growth partners, innovation engines, and customer experience architects.

Publicis Groupe: Strategic Investments and Expansion

Publicis Groupe has been undergoing a strategic transformation for the better part of a decade. From the outside, it might look like a steady drumbeat of acquisitions and restructures, but from the inside, it's clear: Publicis is building a different kind of holding company—one engineered not just for integration but for intelligence.

It started with the landmark acquisition of Sapient in 2014, which gave Publicis a solid foundation in digital consulting and technology. Then came Epsilon in 2019, a data juggernaut that gave it proprietary identity graphs and CRM firepower to rival the platforms. And since then, Publicis has doubled down on technology, with investments in AI, commerce, and analytics.

But now there is a new phase—one rooted in cultural intelligence and influencer power. The acquisition of Downtown Paris, a boutique production house focused on beauty and luxury, was not just about adding creative flair. It was about embedding deeper into the style-conscious, high-touch industries where brand storytelling is everything. Alongside that, Publicis snapped up Influential, one of the top influencer marketing platforms, bringing automated creator discovery and campaign management into the heart of its offering. This was followed by The Mars Agency, a premier retail agency, and Lotame, a strong identity agency match to Epsilon.

Unlike the traditional model of merging agency brands, Publicis has sought to create a modular ecosystem. Clients like Nestlé, L'Oréal, Samsung, and McDonald's have come to rely on "Power of One"—a structure that breaks down silos and assembles bespoke agency teams based on need, not legacy. Each account becomes a constellation of talent—some from Saatchi, some from Leo Burnett, some from Digitas or Starcom—all tied together by unified reporting and a single commercial contract.

Publicis's approach stands in contrast to WPP's custom model with Coca-Cola. It's less about building a new entity and more about choreographing existing pieces. Think jazz ensemble versus symphony orchestra. It's not that one is better—it's about fit. For brands seeking plug-and-play scale with centralized data, Publicis has built an impressive engine. And as the lines between content, commerce, and conversion continue to blur, that engine might be exactly what many marketers need.

The stock market, along with new business league results, suggests that this course so far has been the right one. The holding company has topped R3's new business tracking for the last three years, and its stock price has doubled. The challenge for Publicis Groupe is maintaining that momentum and getting all the individual pieces into a cohesive structure.

The Omnicom and Interpublic Merger: A Potential Game Changer

If the rumors—and then the announcement—of the Omnicom and Inter-public merger sent shock waves through the industry, it's because this was more than a business deal. It was the collapse of a long-standing competitive frontier and the potential creation of a marketing superpower unlike anything we've seen before.

Combined, Omnicom and IPG would become the new largest holding company, controlling hundreds of agency brands, tens of billions in billings, and a vast array of global clients across every vertical. Omnicom brings in the heavyweight names like BBDO, DDB, TBWA, and OMG (OMD, PHD, and Hearts & Science). IPG contributes McCann, FCB, MullenLowe, Mediabrands, and a very robust healthcare practice. Each holding company had been building toward a more integrated model in its own right—Omnicom through its practice areas and IPG through Acxiom and Kinesso. But together? The scale is unprecedented.

Internally, the logic is sound. Media buying power increases. Tech stacks can be unified. Talent pools expanded. Externally, the message to clients is clear: "We can do everything—and we can do it globally, seamlessly, and with strategic depth." But there are major risks.

Brand conflicts will multiply. Uniting agency cultures is always harder than it looks. Clients may not want to be lost inside a giant machine. And regulators may raise eyebrows. But make no mistake: This merger, if it proceeds, will reshape how brands think about partnerships. Already, conversations are shifting: "Do I want the best team from the biggest shop or the most bespoke solution from a smaller independent?"

The most immediate impact will be talent. With redundancies inevitable and leadership roles overlapping, the next wave of independents may be founded by those pushed out by the merger. Just as the Publicis-Omnicom merger fell through in 2014 due to cultural mismatches, this new alliance will need to balance ambition with humility. Size alone won't guarantee success. Integration, vision, and values will.

Gen AI and the Role of Agencies

It's impossible to talk about the future of agency-client relationships without confronting the elephant—or rather, the algorithm—in the room: generative AI. For years, automation had been nibbling at the edges of marketing: programmatic media, dynamic creative optimization, A/B testing on steroids. But gen AI is different. It doesn't just optimize. It creates.

From ChatGPT to Midjourney to Sora, AI tools are becoming cocreators. They can write headlines, generate visual assets, edit video, synthesize research, and even simulate campaign results. Agencies are already building internal gen AI labs, while start-ups are selling AI-produced content at a fraction of agency costs. The question is no longer "Will AI change marketing?" It's "How fast, and how deeply?"

Some fear this will render agencies obsolete. Why pay millions for creative work when a prompt can get you a hundred variations in seconds? But that's a shallow read. What AI produces is content—not necessarily brand, strategy, or breakthrough thinking. Creativity, in the context of marketing, isn't just making things—it's making meaning. And meaning requires understanding culture, emotion, human insight.

What AI *will* do is dramatically shift the value equation. Marketers and agencies who rely on AI for volume and speed will win on efficiency. But those who pair AI with storytelling, purpose, and humanity will win on resonance. Already, agencies are reframing roles. Strategists are prompt engineers. Creatives are curators. Planners are trainers. Media teams are building models that forecast in-market performance before a single dollar is spent.

We're also seeing new tensions emerge. Who owns the output of a prompt? What happens when a brand's AI outputs infringe on copyrighted content? How do agencies build business models when time-based billing breaks down?

The most progressive clients are addressing this head on. Some have internal AI ethics boards. Others are hiring agency AI partners not for deliverables but for governance, training, and innovation. It's a shift from output to enablement.

In the near future, expect to see AI used most powerfully in insight generation, scenario planning, and hyperpersonalization. The best campaigns won't just be creative. They'll be cocreated—by humans with vision and AI with velocity.

Marketing will never be the same. But maybe it was never supposed to be. As always, it's not about the tools. It's about what we do with them.

The New Frontier of Partnership

The world of marketing agencies is evolving faster than ever before. What hasn't changed is the need for partnership. But the definition of partnership is changing. It's no longer about just outsourcing execution. It's about cocreating value. It's about building ecosystems that flex, adapt, and scale. It's about choosing the right model for the moment and having the courage to evolve it when the moment shifts.

"I'm a huge believer in partnership and I don't want to be draconian," says Lenovo's Emily Ketchen. "I don't want to be the 'client.' I want a partner. I want to be challenged. Agencies are experts and the biggest mistake that people make is not taking that expertise seriously. Great partners don't just deliver—they elevate."

"Agencies are an extension of our team in so many ways," says Mastercard's Cheryl Guerin. "It's a strategic partnership. It's natural to have them collaborating with us all the time. We do this within marketing and communications, but we also bring our agencies, teams and cross-functional business partners together all the time, from brainstorming all the way to execution."

Whether you're a marketer at a global brand, a founder building from scratch, or a strategist inside a boutique agency—the same truth applies: Marketing doesn't happen in a vacuum. It happens at the intersection of inside and outside, vision and execution, strategy and soul. But let's now look even deeper into the DNA of the agency-marketer relationship by exploring not just structures but human behavior, misalignment moments, and lessons from the most iconic partnerships that worked—and failed.

When It Works: A Deeper Dive into Brand-Agency Symbiosis

The best partnerships in marketing resemble the best creative collaborations in music or film—an understanding of mutual strengths, shared language, and a balance of trust and challenge. Take Nike and Wieden+Kennedy. Since 1982, this partnership has given us "Just Do It" as well as Colin Kaepernick, Serena Williams, and Tiger Woods narratives that shaped culture. Why has it lasted? W+K never acts like a vendor—it behaves like a co-owner of the brand. And Nike, while famously demanding, lets its agencies get close to its athletes, culture, and product teams.

This is in stark contrast to relationships that become purely transactional. One global CPG brand (we won't name names) once asked its media agency to deliver "innovation" within a three-month contract with weekly check-ins, no access to internal data, and capped fees. The result? High churn, low morale, and a parade of underwhelming ideas. Agencies can't deliver breakthrough work without trust—and time.

Working With Versus Buying From

One of the hardest shifts for many marketers to make is seeing agencies as true partners rather than as vendors. Procurement often treats agency selection like buying office furniture—lowest bid wins, with bonus points for value adds. But marketing is not a commodity. Great strategy, insight, and creativity are not line items—they're outcomes of collaboration.

Smart clients know this. They embed agencies early, include them in business planning, and reward not just output but impact. Increasingly, we're seeing marketers move toward performance-based compensation models—tying agency bonuses to metrics like brand lift, customer acquisition cost, or market share gain. Done right, this aligns incentives. Done wrong, it just adds pressure without clarity.

Global Complexity: Regional Realities

Another dimension that can make or break agency relationships is geography. What works at global HQ may not resonate in Jakarta, São Paulo, or Nairobi.

That's why many brands now adopt a "glocal" approach—global consistency with local customization. But executing this is hard.

"We provide detailed briefs on the challenges," says Sony Interactive Entertainment's Eric Lempel. "As the work starts to develop, we have a good system in place that allows us to reach out to all of our territory leaders around the world to get their feedback. The feedback we receive helps further shape the final work that is deployed."

One European beverage giant created a centralized brand platform and expected every market to use the same creative assets. Local teams resisted. Sales dipped. Eventually, it moved to a hybrid model—central strategy, core creative, and locally adapted executions with input from regional agencies. The results? Rebound in market share and much better alignment.

Independent Agencies: The New Revolution?

While holding companies dominate headlines, the rise of independent agencies is reshaping the market. Shops like Mother, Mischief USA, Gut, and Uncommon have won huge accounts by offering something many clients crave: authenticity, agility, and undivided attention. They're not beholden to shareholder margins or network politics. They pick clients as much as clients pick them.

That said, they face different challenges—scaling globally, offering deep data services, or competing with the price leverage of big networks. Still, their cultural edge and creative freedom often win out. And in a world where brand differentiation is everything, these wild cards offer a powerful counterpoint to the big five.

Not Just Creative but Consultative

What if the agency of tomorrow looks less like an ad shop and more like a business consultancy with a creative heart? Increasingly, agencies are asked to help with customer experience, e-commerce, sustainability communications, and even internal culture. In response, many are hiring strategists from McKinsey, UX designers from Google, and technologists from Amazon.

Agencies are no longer measured just by how clever their campaigns are but by how clearly they can connect marketing to business outcomes. "We created this idea of zombie brands," says Shakir Moin of Coca-Cola. "Now we're applying the same concept to zombie ideas because zombie ideas also drain precious organizational resources."

"Agencies need to strategically differentiate master creative from adaptation," says L'Oréal's Asmita Dubey. "Investing the same energy in both dilutes impact. A more focused approach is crucial in today's fragmented media landscape."

The question isn't "Is this a great ad?" It's "Will this move the needle?" And in that world, creativity becomes a business asset—not a cost center.

Why Some Clients Burn Out Their Agencies

One of the saddest patterns in marketing is the cycle of frequent agency change. A new CMO joins, fires the agency, holds a pitch, hires a new agency, pushes for quick wins, faces headwinds, fires again. This rinse-repeat mentality destroys brand equity and wastes millions. It also signals a deeper issue: lack of internal clarity.

The most successful marketers build long-term relationships with agencies—not out of loyalty but because they've done the work internally to align on what they stand for, what success looks like, and how they want to behave in the market. They brief better. They listen more. And they get better work because their agencies feel safe to challenge them.

Building a Better Brief

It sounds simple, but the quality of a marketing brief can predict the quality of work that follows. Many marketers struggle to articulate what they really want, leaving agencies to guess. The best briefs do three things: clearly state the business problem, define success metrics, and inspire. That's it. Not forty-two-page decks, not vague "make it go viral" requests.

A good brief is a gift. It sets the stage for great work. It honors the agency's intelligence. And it saves time and money. One global pharma company now runs internal training on how to brief agencies—and reports a 25 percent improvement in creative satisfaction scores just one year later.

Shared Rituals, Shared Success

Finally, great partnerships are built on rituals. Weekly WIPs. Monthly strategy sessions. Quarterly business reviews. Annual off-sites. It's not just about the work—it's about how you work together. Some clients even colocate agency staff or embed their own marketers in agency pods. One automotive brand holds a joint creative awards day every quarter—client and agency teams nominating and celebrating each other's best ideas, regardless of whether they were produced. The result? Higher morale, better retention, and stronger output.

Chapter 7
Tools of the Trade:
Marketing's Other Muscle

There was a time when technology was someone else's problem. If the website broke, we called IT. If a media agency wanted a new dashboard, we signed a change order. And if we needed analytics, we hoped someone from finance would "pull a report." Technology was the plumbing. Marketing was the water. But marketing today doesn't just *use* technology—it runs on it. "Beauty tech is revolutionizing our industry," says L'Oréal's Asmita Dubey. "We're embracing AI, automation, and data analytics to enhance efficiency and effectiveness, while never losing sight of the human touch."

Even today, we still meet those who still think "the tech piece" is someone else's job. They've outsourced the ecosystem to vendors, siloed innovation to the digital team, or handed the keys to IT. And then they wonder why it takes six weeks to approve a campaign.

The truth? Technology isn't a support act. It's the infrastructure for everything marketing does—briefing, budgeting, branding, benchmarking. Whether it's managing agencies, running pitches, optimizing content, or measuring performance—tech is in the bloodstream now. And the best marketers? They aren't just learning the tools. They're building marketing *operating systems*—designed for creativity, speed, and scale.

We've entered an era where the tools *are* the team. Martech stacks don't just support your work; they shape how ideas get made, how teams collaborate, and how fast decisions happen. If you want Marketing Inside—want to truly build a function that's strategic, responsive, and growth focused—then you have to embrace the fact that technology isn't just helpful. It's fundamental.

From Martech to Growthtech

If you walk into Lenovo today, you won't find just engineers and product managers talking about devices—you'll find marketers talking about data lakes, orchestration engines, and real-time optimization. That's because, like many future-focused companies, Lenovo realized that marketing isn't just a message; it's an engine. And that engine runs on technology.

For years, marketing tech was seen as the digital team's playground—CRM tools, email platforms, maybe a media demand-side platform (DSP) if you were advanced. But in today's operating environment, the stack is the strategy. It's no longer about managing campaigns. It's about managing outcomes.

Lenovo has built a global marketing stack designed not just for visibility but for velocity. It has connected campaign planning, media buying, creative development, and analytics into a single framework that gives its teams the agility to respond in real time to business needs. It's not just software—it's a system for decision-making.

Adobe, of course, has taken this to a different level—because it is selling the very tools marketers use to build these systems. But what makes Adobe's own marketing operation world class isn't just access to the tech—it's how it uses it. Under the leadership of its CMO, Adobe transformed its marketing organization into a growth lab. It didn't just plug in tools—it rearchitected how marketing worked. With Adobe Experience Cloud at the center, Adobe created a unified view of the customer journey, allowing for personalized, adaptive content at scale. But the real unlock was cultural—it trained marketers to think like engineers and engineers to think like storytellers.

What Lenovo and Adobe both understand is that technology is no longer a back-office function. It's not an add-on. It's a frontline weapon in the race for relevance. Martech is now growthtech—when used right, it doesn't just make things more efficient; it makes marketing more effective.

The Skills to Thrive with Technology

Let's be clear: Buying the tools is easy. The hard part? Building the stack that works.

A successful marketing tech stack isn't about having every platform Gartner puts in its magic quadrant. It's about designing a system that connects insight to action, creativity to conversion, and people to purpose. That takes more than procurement—it takes vision.

First, marketers need **systems thinking**. It's no longer enough to know what a CRM does or how programmatic media works. You need to understand how it all connects—from first impression to final purchase. The best tech stacks are invisible. They work because they remove friction, not because they add complexity.

Second, marketers need **business literacy**. Every tool in the stack should answer a simple question: "Will this help us grow?" If the answer is fuzzy, you're chasing features, not outcomes. Tech isn't about what's possible—it's about what's profitable.

But here's the twist—this isn't a solo act. Building the right stack means working across IT, finance, procurement, and yes, even legal. You need **cross-functional fluency**. That means showing the CIO how a digital experience platform enhances personalization, convincing finance that attribution isn't just voodoo, and helping procurement see value beyond license fees.

"I think the big battle in a lot of companies is really the relationship between the technology departments and the marketing departments in terms of marketing automation," says Cathay Pacific's Ed Bell. "Who is the rightful owner of DCO? There's always tension between the automators and the creators."

Of course, challenges come thick and fast.

- Siloed data? Integrate before you implement.
- Skill gaps? Upskill your team. Train marketers like product managers.
- Vendor sprawl? Own the road map. Let partners plug in, not lead.
- Shiny-object syndrome? Don't buy tech to solve indecision. Start with a problem, and then find the tool.

The marketers who thrive today aren't just tech savvy—they're stack smart. They know the tools don't create impact by themselves. It's how you stitch them together. It's how you bring them inside. And most importantly, it's how you make them work in service of great ideas, not instead of them.

Lenovo: Building a Stack for Speed and Storytelling

When Emily Ketchen became CMO of Lenovo's Intelligent Devices Group, she didn't just inherit a global brand—she inherited a marketing machine stretched across geographies, languages, and legacy systems. For a company selling one in every four PCs worldwide, speed and scale weren't just aspirations. They were survival.

But Ketchen knew the challenge wasn't launching more campaigns. It was connecting them.

Her first move? Rewiring the system from the inside. That meant building a tech stack that could support real-time global storytelling—without losing local relevance. At the heart of it was orchestration: connecting campaign planning, creative development, media delivery, and analytics into a single, agile framework.

The goal wasn't to automate marketing. It was to liberate it.

With support from internal data teams and a restructured agency model, Ketchen's team deployed tools that did more than push content—they pulled insight forward. A centralized marketing cloud gave global teams visibility into asset performance, while automation helped local teams personalize at speed.

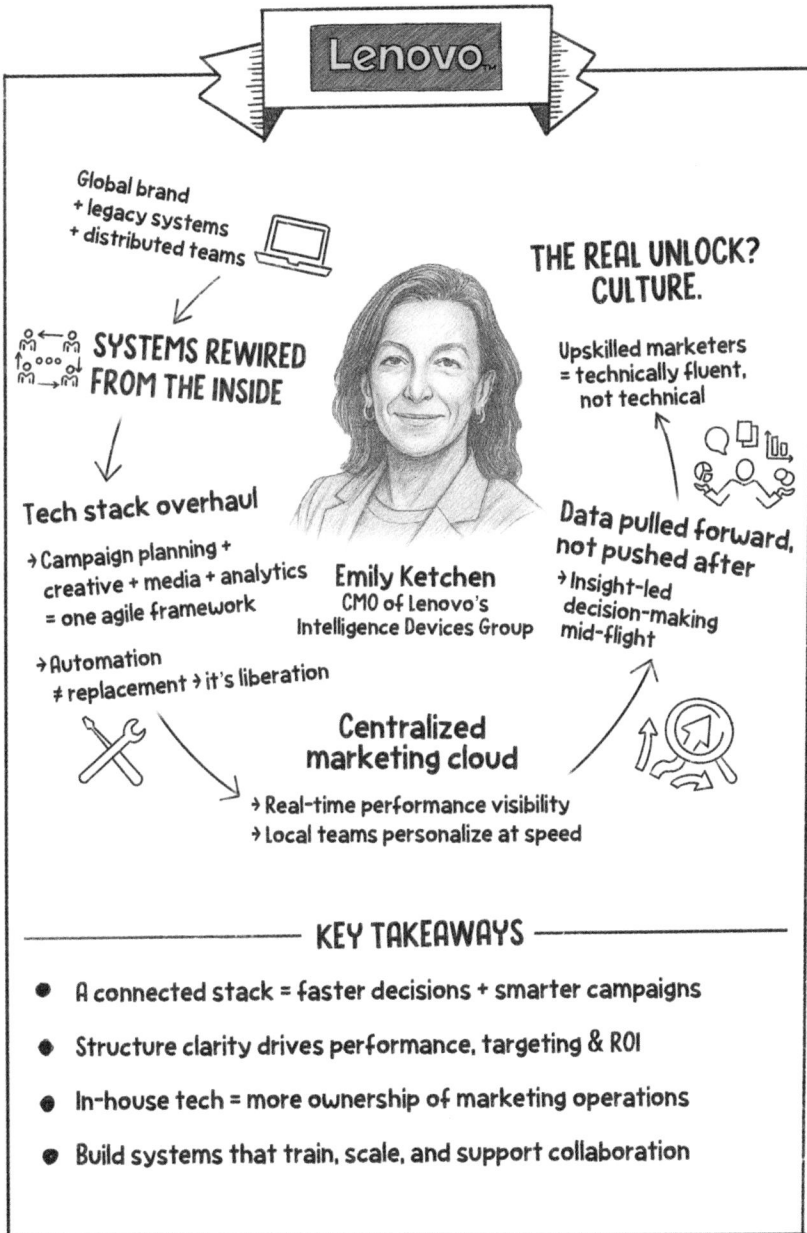

Lenovo.

Global brand
+ legacy systems
+ distributed teams

SYSTEMS REWIRED FROM THE INSIDE

Tech stack overhaul

→ Campaign planning +
creative + media + analytics
= one agile framework

→ Automation
≠ replacement → it's liberation

Emily Ketchen
CMO of Lenovo's
Intelligence Devices Group

Centralized marketing cloud

→ Real-time performance visibility
→ Local teams personalize at speed

THE REAL UNLOCK? CULTURE.

Upskilled marketers
= technically fluent,
not technical

Data pulled forward, not pushed after

→ Insight-led
decision-making
mid-flight

KEY TAKEAWAYS

- A connected stack = faster decisions + smarter campaigns
- Structure clarity drives performance, targeting & ROI
- In-house tech = more ownership of marketing operations
- Build systems that train, scale, and support collaboration

But the real unlock? Culture. Ketchen invested in upskilling marketers—not to become techies but to become technically fluent. Marketers learned to ask better questions of data, push back on performance noise, and collaborate more closely with sales and product teams.

Here's one example: During a major product launch, real-time data flagged underperformance in a key region. Instead of waiting for postmortem reports, the team adjusted creative, redistributed budget, and optimized content mid-flight—saving the campaign and exceeding ROI targets.

Under Ketchen's leadership, Lenovo didn't just modernize its stack—it rewired its mindset. Technology became less about automation and more about acceleration. In her words, "Marketing isn't just about awareness anymore. It's about connection, intelligence, and impact—and we've built the tech to deliver that at scale."

Key takeaways:

- A connected stack enables faster decision-making, more responsive campaigns, and tighter alignment.
- Structural clarity leads to smarter targeting, better performance, and clearer ROI.
- Prioritize control over cost; in-house tech when you want greater ownership of marketing operations.
- Create a system that trains skill, builds capability, and supports collaboration.

Beware the Data Rich, Poor in Application

We once worked with a global CPG client who proudly told us, "We have over two hundred dashboards." The room went quiet. Not because we were impressed—but because we knew what that really meant. They weren't looking at two hundred dashboards. They were drowning in them.

"Data is very important, but I think data is an answer to a problem," says Mukul Deoras of Colgate-Palmolive. "Data is not a solution in itself. Its key challenge is defining the problem. Data and analytics are the tools that help you create a marketing strategy. Data and analytics are not the market strategy."

Data is the oil—it powers the machine. But without the engine, the drive, the decision-making muscle behind it, it's just slick, untapped potential. Every marketer today says they're "data driven." But what are they actually *doing* with it? Are they using it to shape creative? To optimize media in real time? To inform strategic decisions at the top table? Or are they just pulling reports and praying for clarity?

Let's be honest—most organizations don't have a data problem. They have an *application* problem.

Take McDonald's as a counterexample. In 2019, it made an unexpected move: It bought a machine learning company, Dynamic Yield, for over $300 million. Why? Because it didn't want to just *have* data—it wanted to *act* on it. Now, when you pull into a McDonald's drive-through in many countries, the digital menu board changes dynamically. It factors in time of day, weather, trending items, even regional preferences. A Big Mac might be front and center on a Friday night, but a breakfast wrap takes the spotlight on a chilly Monday morning. That's not just personalization—it's data applied at speed and scale. McDonald's didn't just collect insights. It *engineered decisions*.

This is what most marketers miss. The goal isn't to build a data warehouse—it's to build a *marketing nerve center*. A system where insights flow naturally into action. Where your CRM doesn't just house names and emails but tells you when to speak, what to say, and how to say it. Where performance data doesn't sit in a deck—it shapes the brief before the creative even starts.

*We're using econometrics. We are using more appli-
cation of big data to try and set budgets. We're doing
efficiency curves to plot exactly the right amount of
investment in lower funnel. We're quantifying the value
impact of consideration goals because we've done our
own econometrics. What's interesting about that you
need to have a different conversation with revenue
management and sales, and this is good.*

—Ed Bell, Cathay Pacific

This shift takes guts. Because data often tells us things we don't want to hear. That the campaign we loved didn't land. That the agency isn't hitting the mark. That our "gut feeling" needs a reality check. The best marketers aren't just data informed—they're data honest.

And let's not forget: Collecting data is easy. Earning it is hard. Customers don't want to be "tracked." They want to be *understood*. The exchange must be clear—value in, value out. When Spotify Wrapped hits each year, millions of users *choose* to share their data story, because it reflects who they are. That's not surveillance—that's self-expression. So yes, data is the oil. But you still need the engine. You still need the driver. And you still need to know where you're going. Otherwise, you'll just be another marketer with two hundred dashboards—and nowhere to go.

Glanbia: Using Technology to Connect, Personalize, and Perform

Glanbia might not be a household name, but chances are its brands—like Optimum Nutrition and SlimFast—are sitting on the shelves (or in the gym bags) of millions of consumers worldwide. What sets Glanbia apart isn't just product quality. It's how it uses technology to connect with consumers in ways that are personal, timely, and deeply relevant.

Facing fierce competition in the health and wellness space, Glanbia recognized that mass marketing wouldn't cut it. Consumers were no longer looking for generic messages—they wanted personalized advice, tailored product recommendations, and real-time support. That's where technology stepped in.

Glanbia invested heavily in building out a modern martech stack that could support one-to-one engagement at scale. Using platforms like Salesforce Marketing Cloud and Adobe Experience Manager, it created a seamless ecosystem that connected web behavior, purchase data, and CRM insights across markets. This allowed it to send personalized offers, fitness content, and product education based on an individual's goals—whether it was bulking up, slimming down, or staying balanced.

But it didn't stop at email. Glanbia extended personalization to digital media, e-commerce, and loyalty programs—creating a connected experience that followed the consumer across their journey. A gym goer browsing protein powders today might get a targeted Instagram ad tomorrow, followed by a recipe video via email the next morning.

"Technology can be a huge enabler," says Global Chief Brand Officer Colin Westcott-Pitt. "The challenge is you can sometimes end up with people going in different directions because they have different starting points, knowledge and belief systems. Up-front senior-level alignment on ambition and then setting up a structure that can make things happen quickly are pretty important to success."

Crucially, Glanbia brought much of this capability inside. It built in-house teams to manage data strategy and performance media, giving it more control and faster response times. The result? Better ROI, stronger customer relationships, and a brand experience that feels more like a coach and less like a megaphone. For Glanbia, technology isn't just infrastructure—it's intimacy at scale. It's how a global brand acts local, personal, and human—even when talking to millions.

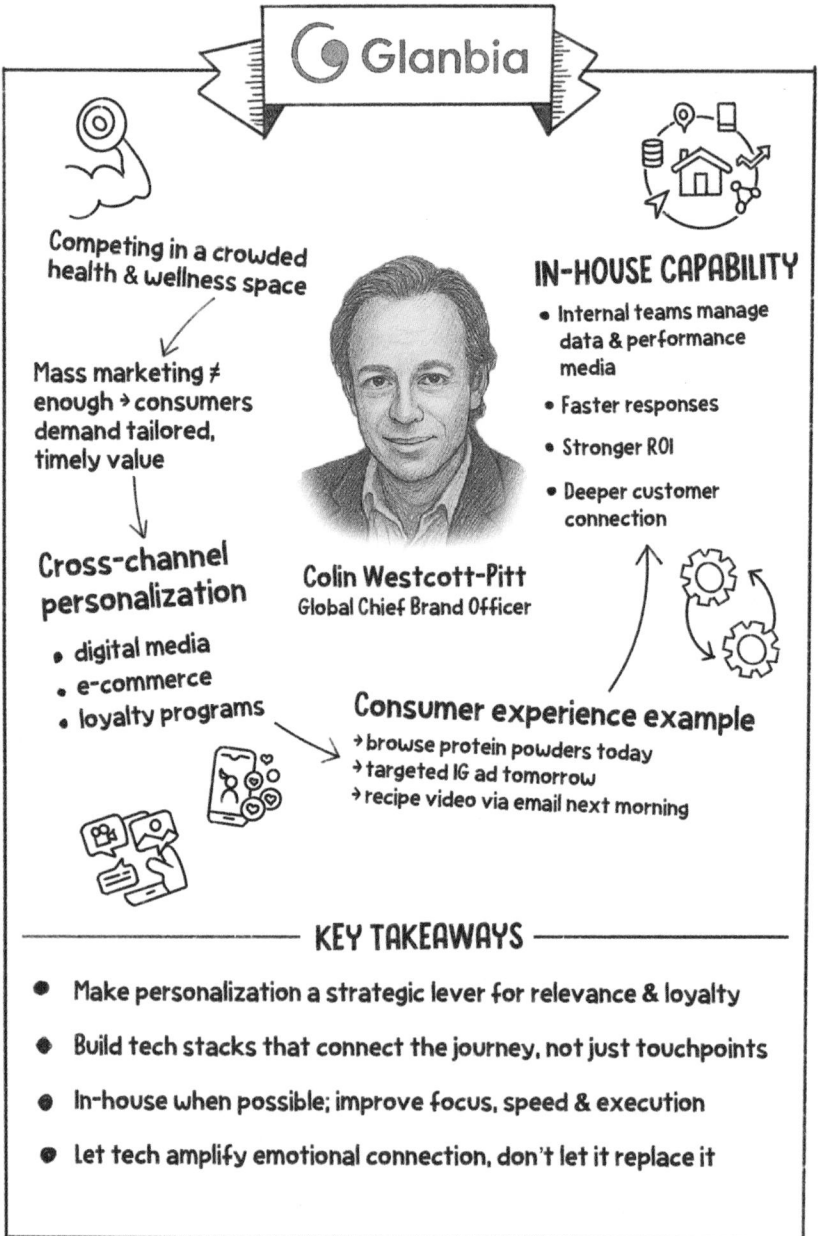

Glanbia

Competing in a crowded health & wellness space

Mass marketing ≠ enough → consumers demand tailored, timely value

Cross-channel personalization
- digital media
- e-commerce
- loyalty programs

Colin Westcott-Pitt
Global Chief Brand Officer

IN-HOUSE CAPABILITY
- Internal teams manage data & performance media
- Faster responses
- Stronger ROI
- Deeper customer connection

Consumer experience example
→ browse protein powders today
→ targeted IG ad tomorrow
→ recipe video via email next morning

KEY TAKEAWAYS

- Make personalization a strategic lever for relevance & loyalty
- Build tech stacks that connect the journey, not just touchpoints
- In-house when possible; improve focus, speed & execution
- Let tech amplify emotional connection, don't let it replace it

Key takeaways:

- Prioritize personalization as a strategic lever for greater relevance and loyalty.
- Ensure your tech stack enables continuity across touchpoints—not just isolated activations.
- Evaluate where in-housing can sharpen focus, improve execution, and reduce dependency on external partners.
- Keep the brand voice and emotional resonance at the center, using tech as an amplifier for human connection.

Bringing Tech Inside: In-Housing Done Right

There's a quiet revolution happening in marketing departments around the world. It doesn't come with a Super Bowl ad or Cannes Lion. No big reveal. No agency gala. Just a quiet shift, one platform login at a time. Marketers are bringing tech inside.

For years, tech sat comfortably on the outside—managed by vendors, optimized by agencies, signed off by procurement. But as the speed of business accelerates, the brands that win are the ones that move fast, iterate faster, and keep control of the narrative. That's hard to do when your data lives in five different agency servers and your digital assets are updated once a quarter.

So marketers have started asking, "What if we built the capability ourselves?" Not to cut costs—but to gain control. Not to eliminate agencies—but to complement them. In-housing isn't a rebellion. It's a realization: If you want to lead, you can't outsource the steering wheel.

Take Bayer, the global pharmaceutical giant. A few years ago, it began an ambitious shift—bringing performance media buying in-house across multiple markets. It wasn't a press stunt. It was a business move. Bayer wanted to reduce time to market, strengthen data ownership, and align media more closely with commercial priorities. But it didn't stop there. Bayer invested heavily in training internal teams, building martech infrastructure, and designing a new operating model that still allowed for agency collaboration—just with Bayer in the driver's seat. Today, it has saved millions in fees, increased transparency, and—most importantly—improved campaign effectiveness by acting faster and learning more from its own data.

That's the blueprint.

But here's the truth: In-housing isn't just a decision. It's a discipline. Here's what you need:

- **Talent** that understands both the art and the architecture—marketers who can brief creative and run DSPs.
- **Technology** that's fit for purpose—modular, interoperable, and actually usable.
- **Process** that's flexible—agile enough to move fast, disciplined enough to stay aligned.
- **Leadership** that's brave—because it's easy to blame a partner. It's harder to own the outcome.

When tech comes inside, so does accountability. So does insight. So does speed. And that's the real win. The smartest marketers today aren't chasing full in-housing as some silver bullet. They're building hybrid models—retaining partners where it makes sense but bringing core capabilities closer to the business. Closer to the customer. Closer to the brand.

When More Tools Mean Less Progress

One of the most common mistakes we see inside marketing organizations is mistaking configuration for collaboration. Somewhere along the way, marketers started believing that the more tools you had, the more sophisticated your operation became. But here's the truth: The more tools you bolt on, the more fragile the system becomes.

Fragmentation kills alignment.

When every team has its own dashboard, every region runs its own CRM, and every agency plugs into a different platform, it doesn't create efficiency—it creates chaos. Decisions get delayed. Insights get lost. Data contradicts itself. Meetings multiply just to "sync." And before long, no one's sure what's real anymore.

The problem isn't just the tech—it's the tech culture. Too many marketers suffer from FOMO: fear of missing out on the next tool that promises ten times results, AI-powered everything, or "real-time" nirvana. So they chase it. They configure. They subscribe. But they rarely stop to ask, "Does this serve how we actually work?" We worked with one global brand that had fourteen different tools being used across six markets just to manage campaign planning. The outcome? More time managing tools than managing the work. That's not transformation. That's paralysis.

The best marketing tech stacks aren't the biggest. They're the clearest. They reflect the actual needs of the scope: the work you do, the way you do it, and the decisions you need to make.

Less dashboard, more dialogue.

"It's really hard when you're trying to change some of your core culture," says Toyota's Mike Tripp. "It's easy to talk about the importance of data and analytics. It's easy to talk about fragmentation of media. It's easy to talk about our audience becoming more diverse. But, if this is true, what are you going to do about it?"

Instead of buying another platform, ask this: "Can our teams actually talk to each other? Can they see the same truth, in the same format, at the same time?" That's collaboration. That's alignment. That's Marketing Inside. Because the right stack isn't the one that impresses a tech analyst. It's the one that helps your team move, decide, and create—together.

Staying Out of the Tech Trap

To avoid the trap of tool sprawl and fragmentation, marketers need to stop shopping like collectors and start building like architects. The goal isn't to have more—it's to have what works.

- **Start with capabilities, not tools:** Don't begin by asking, "What's the best platform?" Start by asking, "What do we actually need to do better?" Define the core capabilities required by your marketing scope—such as campaign planning, creative development, media optimization, measurement—and map tools to those needs, not the other way around.

- **Design an operating model first:** Tools should support your operating model, not dictate it. If your teams work globally but execute locally, your stack needs to support collaboration across time zones, markets, and functions. If your process is agile, choose tools that move fast. Build for how your team works—not how the tool demo looks.

- **Appoint a tech steward inside marketing:** Too often, tech strategy is left to IT or procurement. Appoint a marketing team lead or steward who understands both the tools and the work. Someone who asks, "Does this integrate? Will our people use it? Does it improve outcomes?"

- **Prioritize integration over innovation:** Before buying something new, ask if what you have can be improved or integrated. Many problems are solved not by adding a tool but by fixing how tools talk to each other. Simplicity scales—complexity breaks.

- **Establish a "minimum viable stack":** Adopt a mindset of less, but better. Build a minimum viable stack that covers 80 percent of your needs with maximum usability. Test it. Refine it. Add only when a clear gap emerges, not just because a vendor makes a compelling pitch.

- **Measure tool impact like a campaign:** If you wouldn't run a campaign without KPIs, don't run a platform without them. Define success metrics for tools—adoption, speed, impact on work quality—and review regularly. If a tool isn't adding value, decommission it. Ruthlessly.

Sony PlayStation: Playing to Win with Tech-Enabled Marketing

If there's one brand that understands the fusion of culture, content, and community, it's PlayStation. But behind the cinematic trailers and global hype drops is a marketing team that runs like a performance engine—fueled by technology, data, and razor-sharp precision. Sony PlayStation's marketing organization isn't just trying to sell consoles—it's orchestrating a global entertainment platform with millions of fans, dozens of markets, and one constant challenge: staying ahead of the gamer.

To do this, PlayStation has brought technology inside. Its global team leverages an integrated martech stack that connects CRM, digital media, content planning, and real-time analytics into a single view of the player journey. From preorder campaigns to postlaunch engagement, every beat is mapped, measured, and optimized.

One of PlayStation's biggest breakthroughs? Using Adobe Experience Cloud to create personalized experiences across regions. A gamer in São Paulo sees content that reflects local influencers and events. A fan in Tokyo sees promotions tailored to their in-game behavior. Same platform, different playbook.

But what really sets PlayStation apart is how it listens. Using social listening tools and community sentiment analytics, the marketing team monitors fan conversations in real time. Before the launch of *God of War Ragnarök*, it used audience signals—trending content, subreddit behavior, YouTube replays—to shape campaign timing, influencer choices, and creative strategy. This wasn't just responsive marketing. It was informed orchestration.

Importantly, PlayStation's tech is in service of teams. It has built internal capabilities to manage data, creative, and performance in-house—while still maintaining deep partnerships with agencies.

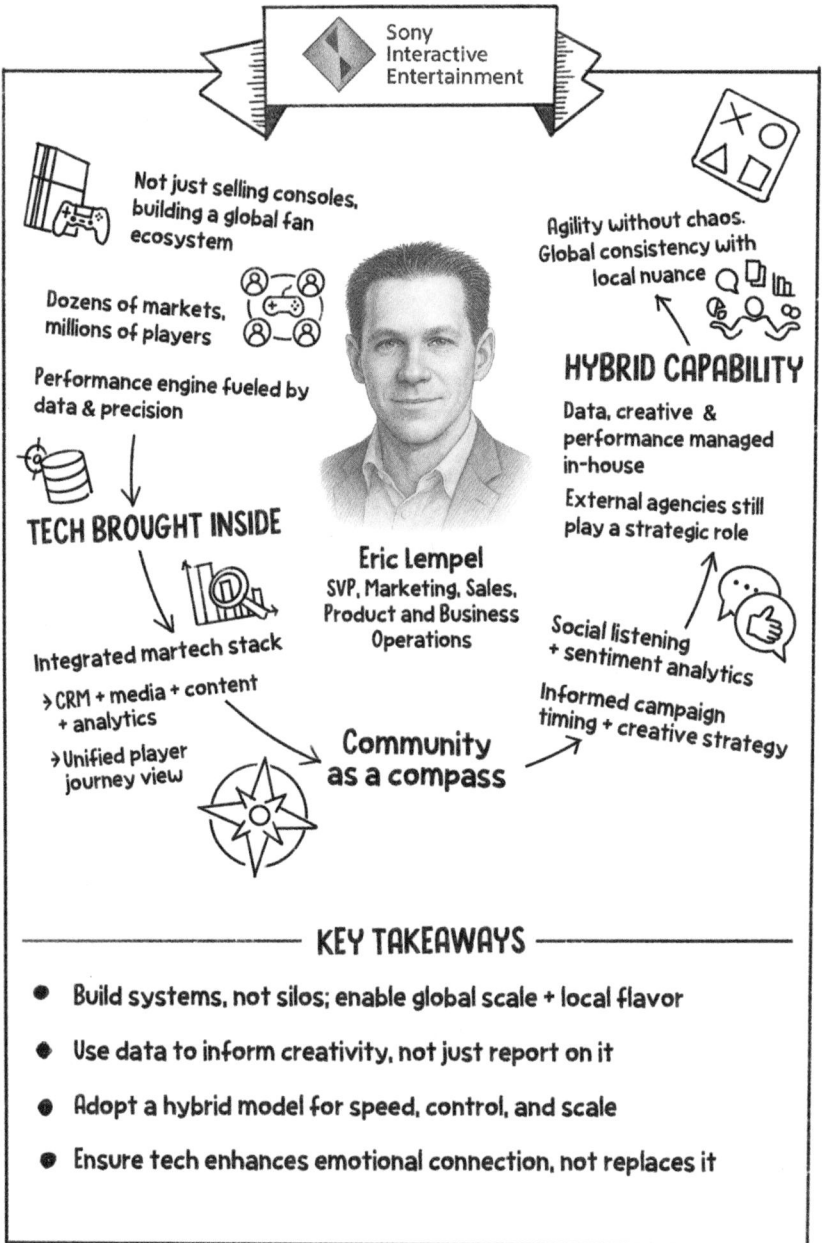

Sony Interactive Entertainment

Not just selling consoles, building a global fan ecosystem

Dozens of markets, millions of players

Performance engine fueled by data & precision

TECH BROUGHT INSIDE

Integrated martech stack

→ CRM + media + content + analytics

→ Unified player journey view

Agility without chaos. Global consistency with local nuance

HYBRID CAPABILITY

Data, creative & performance managed in-house

External agencies still play a strategic role

Eric Lempel
SVP, Marketing, Sales, Product and Business Operations

Social listening + sentiment analytics

Informed campaign timing + creative strategy

Community as a compass

KEY TAKEAWAYS

- Build systems, not silos; enable global scale + local flavor
- Use data to inform creativity, not just report on it
- Adopt a hybrid model for speed, control, and scale
- Ensure tech enhances emotional connection, not replaces it

"We've explored both in-house and outsourced solutions for various needs, says Eric Lempel, Senior Vice President of Marketing, Sales, Product, and Business Operations. "This approach has evolved significantly over the years. I find that for certain levels of creative work, handling it in-house is highly effective, and we've increasingly empowered the in-house team over recent years."

The result? Agility without chaos. Global consistency with local nuance. For PlayStation, technology isn't a gimmick. It's a growth platform. It's how it launches faster, markets smarter, and connects deeper with its fans.

Key takeaways:

- Prioritize systems that eliminate silos and enable global consistency with local execution.
- Use data not just to report but to inform creativity.
- Invest in hybrid models that allow for speed, control, and scalability.
- Ensure that technology enhances—not replaces—the emotional connection with your audience.

AI and the Goosebumps Factor: Creativity Powered by Silicon

Inside the best marketing organizations, AI is considered more than a revolution and more than a threat. It taken the place of something else entirely: a *tool*. A powerful, tireless, always-on creative partner. But still—just a partner. AI doesn't replace human imagination. It *amplifies* it. The smartest marketers aren't using generative AI to cut corners. They're using it to create space—to iterate faster, test more bravely, and personalize at scale without sacrificing soul. They're not asking AI to *be* the idea. They're using it to get to the idea faster.

This is the new creative frontier. It's not man versus machine. It's man *with* machine. A brainstorming assistant who never sleeps. A creative director who speaks in algorithms but listens with precision. A strategist who can process every consumer touchpoint and distill insights in minutes—not weeks. But here's the catch: The brands that win with AI are the ones that never lose sight of what actually matters—*the human on the other end.*

AI is powerful. But goosebumps still win.

Because no matter how advanced the tool, marketing still lives and dies by its ability to make someone feel something. To be seen. To be heard. To be surprised, delighted, inspired. A prompt can't teach you empathy. A model can't feel your customer's heartbeat. But used right, AI can bring you closer to it. "We strive to create the best, most responsible consumer engagement with beauty," says L'Oréal's Asmita Dubey. "While the mediums evolve, that commitment remains constant."

Look at how brands like Coca-Cola have embraced generative tools—not to replace storytelling but to reimagine it. Its "Create Real Magic" platform invited creators from around the world to codesign assets using AI, powered by OpenAI and Bain. But the output wasn't just tech driven. It was fan driven. Personal. Emotional. It didn't dilute the Coke brand—it brought it to life in more voices, more places, with more heart. That's the opportunity: personalization at scale *without losing personality.* Emotion powered by precision.

AI can help marketers see patterns we miss, surface insights we overlook, and unlock speed we never thought possible. But it doesn't replace the gut feeling. It doesn't replace taste. It doesn't replace that electric jolt when you know the work is good—not because the metrics say so but because it gives you goosebumps. That's still the benchmark. That's still the goal.

Managing AI Within the Marketing Ecosystem

Many organizations are rushing to plug AI into their stack as if it's just another vendor module—drop it in, check a box, move on. But AI is not a fixed-function tool. It's a dynamic, adaptive system that requires context, clarity, and continuous calibration. The real challenge isn't access—it's alignment.

Here's when common problems arise:

- **There's a lack of a clear use case:** AI is deployed before there's a defined problem to solve. Teams chase AI because competitors are or because a vendor promised a ten times return—without anchoring the tech to actual business needs.
- **It's introduced into disconnected data infrastructure:** AI models are only as good as the data that feeds them. When customer data is fragmented across tools, geographies, and agencies, AI becomes a sophisticated guesser, not a strategic engine.
- **It's managed by teams with skill gaps in organizational silos:** Marketers don't always speak AI, and data scientists don't always speak brand. Without translators—people who understand both creativity and computation—AI remains underutilized or, worse, misused.
- **There's an inherent fear of losing control:** There's anxiety about creative authenticity, IP ownership, compliance, and ethical boundaries. These aren't technical problems—they're leadership ones. Without a governance framework, fear paralyzes progress.

Here's how to better manage bringing AI into the marketing toolbox:

1. **Start with a capability map, not a platform:** Once again, we come back to the fundamental approach of making decisions based on the needs of the marketing organization. Identify where speed, scale, or

complexity are blocking creativity or performance. Then define the role AI should play—creative assistance, customer insights, personalization, media automation, etc.

2. **Build cross-functional task forces:** Pair marketing leads with data engineers, creatives with AI product managers. Establish shared goals, workflows, and training so teams speak a common language. The aim is to solve problems, not create new ones.

> *"Marketing initiated our AI Governance Council," says Lenovo's Emily Ketchen. "I think we were out there well before anyone else. The AI Governance Council that started in marketing moved into legal, moved into finance, moved into ethics, moved into security, and into all the different parts of our organization. We can't market AI if we don't know what it is. Credibility with AI starts with responsibility."*

3. **Treat AI as a system, not a tool:** Integration isn't just technical—it's cultural. Embed AI within the creative process, the planning cycle, and the customer journey. Measure it not on novelty, but on outcomes.

4. **Create a human-AI operating model:** Define clear guardrails: when AI accelerates, when humans decide, and where collaboration happens. This gives teams confidence—and keeps brand integrity intact.

> *"I really believe that the opportunity is to move from a traditional operating model to more of an AI-centric model," says Toyota's Mike Tripp. "Your limiting factors are financial and people resources. As you scale up and down, they continue to be your limiting factors. But once you adopt technology, then scale actually becomes how you manage scale and learn."*

Designing the Tech Operating System for Modern Marketing

As marketing transforms from a service department into a strategic engine, the need for a cohesive tech operating system (OS) has never been greater. Not just a collection of tools but a structured, scalable system that supports how marketing works, how it learns, and how it grows. Too often, marketers confuse "tech stack" with "tech system." A stack is just a set of tools. A system is how those tools connect—to each other, to the people using them, and to the decisions that drive impact. And without a system, even the best tools end up underused or misaligned.

Here's the truth: The future of Marketing Inside depends not on what tech you have but on how well it reflects and supports your operating model.

Every organization is shaped differently. Some are centralized—one global team driving strategy with local teams executing. Others are decentralized, with each market owning its own budgets, tools, and timelines. Increasingly, we see hybrid models with shared platforms and policies but distributed ownership.

Each model has its own tension:

- **Centralized** teams need systems that ensure visibility and standardization—think dashboards, shared planning tools, unified asset libraries.
- **Decentralized** teams need agility and autonomy—platforms that support local adaptation without losing brand coherence.
- **Hybrid** models need connective tissue—middleware, APIs, and shared data lakes that allow different teams to plug in without breaking the system.

Your tech must reflect these needs—not fight them.

A true marketing OS goes beyond platform licenses. It includes the following:

- **Workflows:** Are briefs, reviews, and approvals standardized or chaotic?
- **Data governance:** Can teams trust the insights, or is everyone running

their own reports?

- **Knowledge sharing:** Do learnings live in decks—or in systems people can actually access and apply?

It's not just about "What tool do we use for this?" It's "Who owns it, how is it used, and does it serve the broader mission?"

"As a healthcare company, we're always going to put safety first, which can mean we are more considered. It's part of our culture," says Haleon's Tamara Rogers. "The safety of our consumers comes first, so we will always ensure there is a 'human in the machine.'

"In terms of AI being involved in the generation of creative, we have a responsible AI approach—both in ensuring accuracy and trust, for example the transparency around whether something has been generated by AI. As we get into more rich audience data, we are taking the opportunity to create synthetic audiences we can 'interview' or test our creative with—and I'm sure this is just the beginning. It's how [we] do it that matters.

"We make sure we've always got an eye on accuracy, transparency and think how we can avoid getting caught in hallucinations and fabrications. We need to build trusted brands—nothing matters more when it comes to your health and that of your loved ones. Here at Haleon, we have a Responsible AI policy and ensure mandatory training for our teams to make sure they are familiar with this and live up to it in their work."

In a world of AI-driven content, real-time media optimization, and global campaign coordination, speed and clarity are everything. You can't afford for decisions to get lost in translation between systems, countries, or teams. A unified tech OS helps marketing act like a single brain—fast, informed, and aligned. Most importantly, it's the foundation for bringing *marketing inside*. When your tools and systems reflect how your team actually works—and are wired to support growth, creativity, and measurement—marketing earns its seat at the table. Not as a cost center. As a capability.

Chapter 8
Performance Management: Driving Accountability and Results

In the 1990s and early 2000s, assessing an agency often boiled down to the next pitch meeting. Formal scorecards were rare. Evaluations happened in boardrooms or over lunch, based on the strength of a deck and the chemistry in the room.

The publication of Kaplan and Norton's *Balanced Scorecard* (1992) introduced the notion of linking marketing activities to strategic objectives through a mix of financial and nonfinancial KPIs. Agencies, once judged on gut feel and creative flair alone, found themselves reporting against market share lifts, brand-health shifts, and ROI on every dollar spent. That shift cracked open the door to a structured view of performance that went far beyond subjective critiques.

Fast-forward to the early 2000s. Web analytics turned every impression, click, and conversion into real-time intelligence. Quarterly business reviews morphed into data-fueled showdowns. It was also the moment "pay-for-performance" models broke through: Agencies could finally earn their keep by hitting lead-gen targets or driving down cost per acquisition rather than by logging hours.

Today's gold standard of agency performance management isn't focused on a static report or a rigid contract. It's a living conversation. It's a dynamic, two-way dialogue where client and agency coauthor solutions, refine strategies on the fly, and build a foundation of empathetic trust. When performance becomes an ongoing partnership rather than a once-a-quarter audit, you don't just measure success—you create it, every single day.

Maintaining the Client-Agency Relationship

The average client-agency partnership now spans nearly seven years (according to a recent ANA/4As *Client-Agency AOR Relationship Tenure* report)—more than double the 3.2-year average of a decade ago. That stretch of time isn't just comfort; it's a runway for performance management frameworks to take root and drive real value.

Tenure ebbs and flows with review practices: Brands that skip mandatory pitches enjoy relationships of over eight years on average, while those enforcing reviews every three years or more often see tenure slip to under six and four years, respectively. Fewer check-the-box reviews mean agencies can focus on optimizing campaigns instead of defending pitches, fueling deeper collaboration and continuous improvement.

And it shows in the work. System1's recent study on "creative consistency" (which includes agency tenure as a key factor) found that brands in the top 20 percent for consistency not only produced higher-rated ads (3.3 stars versus 2.8 and 2.6) but also recorded twice as many instances of profit gain as the least consistent cohort.

Think more broadly about the value of performance management—it's not just about KPIs and deciding whether your agency has earned its bonus. Without fit-for-purpose performance management frameworks, relationships drift into ambiguity, budgets bloat on low-impact activities, and creative brilliance finds itself buried under misaligned objectives. Ultimately, marketers and agencies thrive when they share both risk and reward. Performance management frameworks codify that alignment—laying out what "success" looks like, how it's measured, and how both sides benefit when goals are exceeded.

GEICO and the Martin Agency

I still remember the first time I saw the GEICO gecko—an unlikely spokescreature whose Cockney wit immediately cut through the insurance clutter. That mascot wasn't just a stroke of creative luck; it was the start of a partnership built on deep brand empathy, relentless innovation, and mutual trust.

From day one, the Martin Agency treated GEICO not as a transactional client but as a coauthor of its brand story. Rather than locking down rigid creative guidelines, the agency worked with GEICO to see the business as "a feeling," allowing wiggle room for everything from the cavemen's knowing glances to Will Arnett sparring with the gecko. That flexibility kept each campaign fresh and ensured the work never felt formulaic yet always unmistakably GEICO.

Behind the scenes, the relationship between GEICO and Martin thrived on shared goals and transparency. The teams codified success around measurable lifts in quote starts and policy conversions, flowing data back and forth in real time. When digital channels exploded, Martin's media planners pivoted rapidly—testing new formats and optimizing bids minute by minute—while creative scribes fed insights on tone and humor into every script. That agility cemented confidence on both sides: GEICO knew Martin could deliver, and Martin felt empowered to push bold ideas.

Decades in, the proof is in the numbers: GEICO has kept the Martin Agency on retainer since 1995, one of the longest-standing creative partnerships in the industry. Even when GEICO briefly paused its search for additional agencies this year, it reaffirmed that no other shop understood its voice—and its audiences—quite like Martin.

In the end, their longevity comes down to a shared thesis: Treat performance management as a living dialogue, marry data with bold creativity, and never lose sight of the brand's human spark.

Designing Performance Evaluations That Work

Building a performance-evaluation framework is like planting a partnership garden—you need the right soil, seeds, and ongoing care to see anything bloom. From sixty thousand feet, these are the components of evaluations that work:

1. Select an approach that is right for your business.
2. Agree on a cadence.
3. Codefine "success."
4. Tailor the tools to the work at hand.
5. Build in two-way feedback from day one.
6. Balance data with insight.
7. Design the right incentives.
8. Keep the framework alive.

1. Select an Approach That Is Right for Your Business

When marketers set out to evaluate agency partners, they can choose from a spectrum of performance management tools—each suited to different cultures, strategic priorities, and data maturity levels.

360-degree feedback and self-evaluation: Borrowed from HR best practices, 360-degree assessments invite input from peers, clients, and the agency itself, surfacing blind spots in collaboration and process. Agencies like VML's Connected Media practice lean on these holistic reviews to sharpen teamwork and cultural fit—especially when cocreating across brand, performance, and influencer pods.

KPI dashboards and real-time scorecards: When speed and precision matter—think programmatic buys or e-commerce activations—brands deploy live dashboards tracking cost per acquisition, viewability, or conversion lifts. Coca-Cola's OpenX unit, for example, codeveloped a shared media dashboard with WPP to monitor sales lift, share of voice, and sentiment in near-real time, enabling rapid budget pivots and creative tweaks.

Balanced scorecards and strategic objectives: For organizations tying marketing tightly to corporate strategy, the balanced scorecard remains a gold standard. Over 88 percent of Fortune 500 companies report using it to link financial and nonfinancial KPIs—blending market share growth, brand-health metrics, and internal process indicators into a unified score.

Benchmarking and peer comparisons: Some marketers prefer process benchmarking—comparing their agency's performance against industry best practices on quality, time, and cost. This approach works well for procurement—savvy brands like Unilever, which use external media-rate surveys and creative-quality audits to set realistic targets and reward partners that outperform peers.

Companies select methods based on their goals and operating rhythms: Fast-moving digital teams gravitate to real-time dashboards, while global brands with complex stakeholder maps lean into balanced scorecards. No off-the-shelf evaluation framework is going to work for a marketing organization that wants the best partnerships. The smartest marketers often blend—and evolve—these approaches, ensuring their evaluation framework remains as dynamic as the marketplace itself.

2. Agree on a Cadence

You don't wait until the year's end to ask, "How are we doing?" The moment you sign a new agency agreement—be it for creative, media, digital, or influencer—you should set your first performance checkpoint. Think of it as a "getting to know you" review three months in, when the honeymoon phase fades and real work is underway. By then you'll have data on campaign launches, briefing clarity, and approval cycles, and you can course correct before small irritants become entrenched frustrations.

Once you've cleared that first milestone, shift into a rhythm that balances rigor with agility. Monthly check-ins—light, thirty-minute stand-ups focused on top-line metrics and roadblocks—keep the dialogue fresh and prevent surprises. These touchpoints aren't scorecards; they're fast-moving huddles where you celebrate quick wins, flag underdelivery, and tweak tactics on the fly.

Every quarter, however, it's time for a deeper dive. Block out half a day for a true "business review"—coauthoring dashboards, revisiting your North Star KPIs, unpacking creative performance, and refining your media mix. These sessions should combine hard numbers (cost per acquisition, brand-health lift, funnel velocity) with open-ended feedback on process, collaboration, and innovation. The goal is a living action plan: Retire stale metrics, pilot new tests, and double down on what's working.

Finally, an annual evaluation brings the full leadership team together—marketing, procurement, agency heads—to assess strategic alignment, renew charters, or reset budgets. But by embedding performance conversations every month and every quarter, you avoid the pressure cooker of a single yearly review. You turn performance management from a dreaded audit into an ongoing partnership ritual—where both sides learn faster, adapt sooner, and build the kind of trust that delivers breakthrough work year after year.

3. Codefine "Success"

The secret sauce to great agency relationships isn't a thicker contract—it's how you kick off and maintain a crystal-clear conversation about what success looks like. When expectations are vague, missteps get chalked up to "the agency" or "the client," and trust erodes. By structuring communication around shared roles, two-way feedback, aligned objectives, and concrete action plans, you transform agency relationships from vendor transactions into dynamic partnerships—where every performance conversation drives smarter decisions and fuels faster growth.

Rally the right cast. Invite your top talent, procurement lead, agency leads, and the teams in the trenches to a single kickoff session, and land on one or two truly strategic outcomes—whether it's lifting brand health, driving cost per acquisition below a threshold, or accelerating qualified-lead growth. That shared vision becomes your North Star.

Align on a clear direction from the outset. Nail down the "why" behind each KPI. Spell out not just which metrics matter but how they tie back to your broader brand and business goals. When you align on a clear direction from the onset, every creative sprint, media buy, or PR outreach maps back to the same North Star—eliminating scope creep and squashing competing priorities.

Unilever's "Reward the Best; Don't Push the Rest"

I'll never forget the day Unilever's CMO said, "We need partners, not vendors"—and that simple shift in mindset transformed the way it worked with agencies. Instead of chasing the cheapest pitch, Unilever pioneered a "reward the best; don't punish the rest" model back in 2008, tying agency fees directly to outcomes like market share gains and brand-health improvements.

That performance-first framework did more than sharpen accountability—it built trust. Agencies knew exactly what "success" looked like, and when quarterly reviews rolled around, conversations centered on moving the needle rather than rehashing blame. Underperforming tactics triggered coauthored recovery plans instead of fines, keeping the tone collaborative and focused on solutions. As a result, core partners saw their remits expand—Unilever rewarded deep expertise and agility with longer contracts and bigger briefs.

Today, Unilever's enduring agency partnerships are rooted in three performance management pillars: transparent, shared KPIs; continuous, two-way feedback; and outcome-based incentives that reward long-term growth over short-term fixes. By cocreating metrics, coauthoring action plans, and treating performance as a living dialogue, Unilever has turned once-annual audits into the very engine of its marketing success—ensuring agencies stay invested, innovative, and aligned for the long haul.

When Your Agency Is In-House: AB InBev draftLine

draftLine is AB InBev's in-house creative agency, launched in 2017 to streamline brand building and accelerate go-to-market execution. Embedded within AB InBev's marketing organization, draftLine operates on a seed-launch-sustain model, combining agile creative teams with data-driven performance metrics to drive sales lifts, market share growth, and award-winning campaigns. Its performance framework is bespoke—one part creative rigor, one part business discipline.

From the outset, draftLine didn't float in a vacuum. It was held to a seed-launch-sustain model that tied every campaign back to real sales lifts and market share gains reported in AB InBev's annual results. But raw sales weren't enough. Tracy Stallard, draftLine's founder, introduced a "creative spectrum" tool that benchmarks every idea on both originality and commercial impact—setting clear growth targets for each marketer and pod across regions.

Performance reviews happen weekly in cross-functional "war rooms," where finance, sales, and creative teams huddle over real-time dashboards. These sessions track not only cost per engagement and channel ROI but also test-and-learn metrics—pretesting creative variants to forecast campaign success before launch and then iterating within days based on live data.

Perhaps most telling, AB InBev folded in external benchmarks—like Cannes Grand Prix wins and Effie short listings—into draftLine's scorecard, ensuring that award recognition wasn't a vanity metric but a signal of genuine effectiveness.

By cocreating KPIs with finance and sales, embedding two-way feedback loops, and balancing speed with strategic depth, AB InBev has turned draftLine into a true growth engine—proving that even an in-house agency thrives when held to the highest performance standards.

4. Tailor the Tools to the Work at Hand

A creative brief demands brand-equity measures and "idea potency" judgments, while a media plan needs real-time ecPM and viewability benchmarks. Demand-generation squads will live off funnel-velocity metrics, but influencer and PR partners deserve engagement authenticity scores and tone-weighted share of voice. One size never fits all.

Too often, marketers reach for off-the-shelf scorecards built for procurement or HR and discover too late that they do more damage than good. These generic tools tend to spotlight cost savings, process compliance, and on-time delivery—metrics that completely miss the heart of marketing, where success lives in brand lift, breakthrough ideas, and audience connections. When you grade agencies on transactional measures instead of creative impact, you train them to "play to the form" rather than to surprise and engage your customers.

To avoid these pitfalls, performance evaluations must be custom built for marketing: blending quantitative business outcomes with qualitative insights. Don't lump creative, media, PR, and digital into one generic checklist. **Organize your scorecard by discipline**—rating strategic planning, execution quality, responsiveness, and innovation in each area. **Tie every criterion back to your agreed goals**—whether that's breakthrough ideas, reach efficiency, or sentiment lift.

A Closer Look at Discipline-Specific Criteria

Creative	Performance can't live or die on clicks alone. Anchor evaluations in brand-health indicators—awareness lift, sentiment shifts, even earned media value—and pair them with qualitative "idea potency" scores codeveloped by both sides. Reward agencies for daring concepts that spark buzz, not just safe plays that meet a brief.
Media	This is where precision shines. Build real-time dashboards tracking eCPMs, viewability, and reach against benchmarks you've agreed upon. Layer on cost-per-engagement targets and bonus gates for overdelivery. At the end of each sprint, host a "media huddle" to surface wins, troubleshoot underserving segments, and ramp up investment where it matters most.
Digital/ Demand Gen	Fast cycles demand micro-KPIs—click-through rates, landing-page conversion jumps, funnel-velocity metrics. But don't let the tyranny of daily dashboards blind you: Weave in quarterly business reviews that step back to assess quality of traffic and downstream revenue attribution.
Influencer	Influence thrives on authenticity, not impressions alone. Cocreate metrics like genuine engagement rate (comments, shares, saves) and track downstream impact—traffic, sign-ups, or sales tied back to influencer content. Reward agencies for securing partnerships with niche voices and for content that drives both social proof and business results.
PR	Coverage volume isn't everything. Score performance on share of voice against competitors, tone analysis in key outlets, and the quality of message placement (headline prominence, backlinks, syndication reach). Incentivize agencies to proactively pitch stories that align with your narrative, secure thought-leadership placements, and leverage crisis-management drills into stronger brand credibility.

5. Build In Two-Way Feedback from Day One

A two-way channel of communication builds mutual respect, surfaces hidden roadblocks, and keeps the partnership from drifting into blame. It also keeps agency-versus-client bias in check. It's not uncommon for marketers to assume their own internal processes are flawless while agencies shoulder all the blame for missed targets.

Some marketers shy away from two-way agency evaluations because they worry the mirror might crack the relationship rather than strengthen it. They fear that opening up feedback channels will invite criticism of their own processes—slow approvals, unclear briefs, shifting priorities—and expose gaps in the client team's performance. Without a foundation of trust, that raw honesty can feel more like a blame game than a growth opportunity.

Others dread the politics of reciprocal reviews. As the *Financial Times* has reported, 360-degree feedback processes can be gamed by "handpicked" reviewers or inflated scoring to avoid tension—turning what should be an objective dialogue into workplace chess. Marketers worry that agencies, under pressure to keep the business, will pull their punches—or, conversely, weaponize critiques to win concessions on budget or scope.

Time and resources also play a part. Setting up true two-way sessions—and following through on action items—requires discipline. When teams are already stretched thin, it's easier to default to one-sided scorecards and skip the hard conversations.

To overcome these barriers, brands need to embed two-way feedback into a broader culture of continuous improvement—backed by clear norms (no surprises) and facilitated workshops rather than ad hoc surveys. Only then does agency feedback feel less like a performance review and more like the kind of open, strategic conversation that fuels real creative and business breakthroughs.

AI's Impact on Performance Measurement

For years, creative and media agencies operated in parallel universes: one dreaming up breakthrough ideas; the other obsessing overreach, frequency, and cost efficiency. Their compensation models reflected that divide—retainers for strategy and creative, labor fees and media commissions for execution. But the rise of AI is collapsing those silos and rewriting both performance and pay.

Generative tools can now draft scripts, design banners, and even optimize bids in seconds—leaving brands to ask why they should pay traditional hourly rates for work a machine can accelerate. Yet AI's real impact isn't about replacing people; it's about magnifying purpose. Agencies that lean on automation to free up human talent for higher-order thinking can shift compensation toward outcome-based models, tying fees to the very metrics that matter: brand lift, engagement quality, and incremental sales.

This convergence means creative and media teams must co-own performance. A banner ad isn't just judged on click-through rates; its creative quality and message resonance become part of the same success formula. In practice, this looks like unified dashboards where real-time bid optimizations sit alongside sentiment analysis and A/B test results. Fees then flex with performance—base retainers cover partnership and strategic counsel, while bonuses reward the AI-driven efficiencies and creative breakthroughs that move the needle.

The brands getting ahead embrace this living partnership. They no longer see "creative versus media" but rather "creative through media," where every algorithmic bid and every narrative twist feeds a single story of growth. By aligning compensation with collective performance—and harnessing AI as both tool and catalyst—they've transformed agency relationships into engines of continuous innovation and shared success.

6. Balance Data with Insight

Too often, performance evaluations read like financial statements—rows of hard numbers tracking clicks, impressions, and conversion rates. But marketing lives in the space where data meets emotion, and that's why you need both qualitative and quantitative measures to get the full picture. Quantitative metrics tell you if your campaigns hit traffic and sales targets; qualitative insights explain *why* they did or didn't, surfacing the human responses behind the dashboards.

Imagine celebrating a spike in click-throughs, only to learn through focus group feedback that your creative felt tone-deaf. Without those voice-of-customer nuggets, you risk chasing hollow wins—green lights on the scorecard that mask eroding brand sentiment or missed creative opportunities. Conversely, qualitative praise—"the storytelling resonated deeply"—rings hollow unless you can anchor it in lift tests or cost-per-engagement improvements.

Lean too heavily on numbers and you'll slip into vanity-metric bias, optimizing for the easiest KPIs rather than the ones that truly move the needle. Dashboards overflow with data, but buried in the noise lie the real strategic levers—brand-health shifts, idea potency, even stakeholder sentiment—that only narrative feedback can uncover.

By weaving quantitative rigor with qualitative color—from campaign analytics to candid agency and customer commentary—you turn evaluations into living conversations. You catch subtle misfires before they become headline fiascos, and you celebrate creative breakthroughs not just because the numbers rose but because you understand the story behind the rise.

7. Design the Right Incentives

Marketing's compensation landscape is shifting from fixed retainers to dynamic, outcome-linked bonus structures—and it's reshaping how agencies innovate and invest in client success. According to the World Federation of Advertisers' *Global Agency Remuneration Trends* report, a growing proportion of clients now blends traditional fees with performance-based incentives, rewarding agencies for hitting agreed business KPIs rather than simply logging hours.

Brands like Unilever and Coca-Cola have led the way, codifying "growth indices" that blend market share gains, brand-health lifts, and efficiency metrics into their bonus formulas—giving agencies both the clarity of targets and the upside for overachievement.

Agencies respond. When a meaningful slice of fees is contingent on hitting shared benchmarks—whether cost-per-acquisition thresholds, incremental sales lifts, or social-engagement goals—they pour resources into real-time analytics, agile testing, and cross-discipline collaboration. Yet the smartest bonus schemes balance upside rewards with joint recovery plans for underperformance, sidestepping punitive traps that can stifle creativity.

The result? Partnerships grounded in shared risk and reward, where agencies feel empowered to push bold ideas precisely because they know their efforts translate directly into tangible—and measurable—value.

8. Keep the Framework Alive

We've journeyed from intuition to independent benchmarking, from scorecards to pay for performance, and now to real-time, AI-enabled continuous improvement. And frankly, there's no turning back. The client-agency relationships that thrive will be those that treat performance management not as a once-a-quarter audit but as the very engine of their partnerships.

Revisit metrics each quarter, retire stale KPIs, pilot new tests, and infuse AI insights wherever possible—whether that's using machine learning to predict the top-performing creative variant or surfacing emerging micro-influencers. When your evaluation tool feels as dynamic as the market, you'll cultivate an agency relationship rooted in trust, creativity, and continuous growth.

Chapter 9
The Six Secrets to Great Marketing

Marketing today is both an art and a discipline under siege.

We live in an age where attention is scarce, data is overwhelming, and CMO tenure is shrinking. Yet, the brands that rise above the noise still manage to unlock something timeless and powerful. They practice good marketing. Not perfect marketing. Not fashionable marketing. But consistently good marketing. And beneath the noise, there are six secrets that help them do so.

In this chapter, we explore these six secrets through stories, strategies, and the real-world lessons of brands that are making it happen. From Tokyo to Toronto, from Mumbai to Minneapolis, these lessons are universal—but how they're applied reveals the craft of great marketers. These secrets don't belong on coffee mugs or PowerPoint decks. They belong in the bloodstreams of companies that care about growing the right way.

Hire Giants

David Ogilvy once said, "If each of us hires people who are smaller than we are, we shall become a company of dwarfs. But if each of us hires people who are bigger than we are, we shall become a company of giants." It's advice more relevant now than ever. In a marketing world obsessed with tools, dashboards, and AI prompts, we've sometimes lost sight of the essential truth that people still make the biggest difference.

"The secret of marketing is not just optimizing the four Ps. There's another P—Passion," says Mukul Deoras of Colgate-Palmolive. "Passionate marketers build a strong marketing organization. People need to love marketing. When you build the passion, it will happen. When there's no passion, it's just a job."

At R3, we've had a front-row seat to the transformation of marketing across continents—and the best transformations always started with one or two giant hires. These were not always the most obvious candidates. Often, they were from different industries—anthropologists hired to decode behavior, musicians brought in to reimagine sonic branding, and retail experts who turned supply chains into brand stories.

At Coca-Cola, Shakir Moin exemplified this thinking. When he took the reins for North American marketing, he didn't change agencies or overhaul processes at first. Instead, he focused on people. He built what he called the Goosebumps group—a collection of diverse thinkers empowered to challenge each other, to share, and to surprise. "The Goosebumps routine is to meet every fortnight," says Moin. "We don't review creative for approvals. We review creative to learn and constantly push ourselves." The result wasn't a top-down model but a network of mutual respect that turned creative reviews into goosebump-generating sessions.

Over at Mastercard, Cheryl Guerin has made a career out of hiring people with elasticity—those who could flex between data and emotion, art and science. When Mastercard leaned into experiential marketing, it wasn't because someone built a nice deck. It was because there were leaders brave enough to step away from legacy metrics and embrace the unknown. "The secret to marketing is about constant inspiration," she says. "We get the best out of people because we do things that people truly care about. It's passion driven and it's purpose driven—people are inspired to do great work. Build a culture of collaboration, curiosity, test and learn, and entrepreneurship—that's when the magic happens."

And Sony PlayStation? After a misstep with PlayStation 3 that was driven largely by internal engineering challenges, the company made the call to hire leaders who understood gamers first. The PlayStation 4's messaging, tone, and content were all gamer driven, with teams immersed in online communities, subreddit AMAs, and Twitch live streams. The culture shifted—and so did sales.

Hiring giants isn't about pay bands or MBAs. It's about taste. Judgment. Courage. And the humility to let them lead. If you want extraordinary marketing, start with extraordinary marketers.

Go MaaS, Not Mass

We explored this in detail earlier—but it deserves deeper treatment. Marketing as a Service (MaaS) is more than a model. It's a mindset. A marketing ecosystem where scale doesn't mean sameness and customization doesn't require chaos.

The old playbook said centralize everything, push out assets, and hope for relevance. MaaS says modularize, orchestrate, and empower. "We can buy anything. What we cannot buy is marketing competitive advantage," says Colgate-Palmolive's Mukul Deoras. Lenovo embraced this when it realized the need to market in both Shenzhen and São Paulo with equal intelligence. It set up regional marketing hubs—MaaS engines—that combined strategy, insight, production, and deployment. These centers didn't just push campaigns—they prototyped, tested, and learned at market speed.

L'Oréal took it even further. Its internal creative studio became a sandbox. By allowing internal talent to work alongside influencers, freelancers, and agencies, it created an agile team that could spin up product launches in weeks, not quarters. The Luxe division used MaaS to launch global campaigns with local adaptability. Same fragrance. Same theme. But the storytelling felt native everywhere it appeared.

Cathay Pacific's recovery after the pandemic is another master class. By outsourcing customer storytelling and giving customers cocreation power, it made loyalty program members feel like brand authors. This wasn't outsourcing—it was outpartnering.

MaaS allows you to move at the speed of relevance. It gives you a level of authenticity that reflects what actual consumers want from a brand—not to be sold to, but to engender utility and capability. You gain agility, creative elasticity, and efficiency. But it requires structure. Clear roles. Tight briefs. And an operating model built for iteration, not perfection.

Invented Here Syndrome

We know what "not invented here" means—but few organizations talk about the dangers of "invented here syndrome." It's when the good ideas that originate inside the company stay stuck inside, unable to travel across functions, silos, or borders.

It's very closely related to what we call "MCA—The World's Largest Agency." MCA is not a new holding company you haven't heard of. It stands for "My Cousin's Agency"—and you see it with every brand manager and every local office. A few years ago, we took on a new global CPG company with one thousand marketing people. It also had one thousand agencies. One single global brand had six different positionings, depending on the region or market it was in.

This is where the real waste in marketing lies.

At Glanbia, the global nutrition giant, they noticed that marketing teams across regions were building similar programs without ever talking to each other. Some were brilliant, but they never left their country of origin. So Glanbia launched the "Global Sparks" program: Every campaign had to be uploaded to a central hub, tagged with learnings, and presented on a monthly internal webinar. Suddenly, Ireland was borrowing from India. The United States was adapting campaigns from Spain. The wheel stopped getting reinvented.

Toyota created cross-regional sharing pods. Its approach—rooted in kaizen—was not just operational but cultural. Dubai and Jakarta may be miles apart, but the lessons on hybrid vehicle campaigns became shared knowledge. It wasn't just efficiency—it was brand coherence.

L'Oréal's internal Cannes-style contest encouraged pride and internal competition. The real benefit? A sense of identity and shared ambition across brands and regions. It gamified knowledge sharing.

Invented here syndrome often starts with good intentions: Protect quality; manage risk. But left unchecked, it creates islands. Good marketers are bridge builders. They ensure that good ideas don't get crushed in the department where they were born.

Data Dies in Darkness

We live in a time where data is marketed as a panacea. Every deck begins with charts. Every vendor promises insights. But the reality inside marketing teams is often very different. Data is fragmented. Locked in silos. Owned by departments. Misinterpreted. Or worse—ignored.

"Data is the new oil," they say—but it's a crude oil that comes out of the ground and needs to be refined. Are you refining it? Or just using it as a crutch?

The phrase "data dies in darkness" isn't just poetic—it's practical. If your data isn't seen, shared, and made actionable, it's useless. Haleon, which spun out from GSK Consumer Health, recognized this as a core marketing challenge. Its first step wasn't to buy new tools—it was to change behaviors. It built what it called "transparency pods": cross-functional teams that included data scientists, creative leads, and media buyers. These pods met weekly—not just to review numbers but to ask better questions. "Why did this campaign underperform with women over thirty-five? What can we test next week?"

At Colgate, regional teams get a biweekly report that is part dashboard, part conversation starter. It flags anomalies—like interest in oral care rising among foodies in Brazil—and asks for hypotheses. Data here is not the final word. It's the opening line.

Sony PlayStation's marketing team doesn't wait for sales dips to course correct. They use gameplay data to forecast churn and spike interest. When behavior shows players dropping off certain games, marketing is briefed. Promotions, community engagement, and even downloadable content become proactive—not reactive.

Data must be democratized. That means investing not only in tools but in training. Haleon instituted a "data storytelling" program where junior marketers learned to build narratives from dashboards. Because raw data is intimidating. Stories invite action.

Marketing is intuition plus information. If the latter is buried or ignored, you're only guessing. Shine light. Share widely. Ask better questions. Only then will the data live.

You Can't Move What You Can't Measure

There's an old engineering saying: "You can't control what you don't measure." In marketing, the corollary is simple: You can't improve what you don't track, and you can't scale what you don't understand. Too often, marketers chase metrics that feel good—likes, shares, even impressions—without tying them to outcomes. But business leaders don't pay for sentiment. They pay for movement.

At Toyota, every general manager is held accountable for brand lift and purchase intent, not just volume sales. Marketing KPIs are part of leadership scorecards. It changes behavior. The marketing team becomes a strategic engine—not a support function.

Mastercard doesn't use just one KPI—it uses layers. Awareness is tracked, yes, but so is emotional resonance. Its "Priceless" platform is scored not only by recall but by emotional engagement and action triggers. It uses neuroscience, not just surveys.

Coca-Cola piloted a new approach to its Fanta rebrand. Thirty pieces of content were launched. Within ten days, performance data was in. Underperformers were culled. Winners were given more media. It was Darwinian—but backed by real-time insights.

"Imagine the transformational shift," says Coca-Cola's Shakir Moin. "We are making marketing as something that is attributed to behavioral change. It's marketing that is data-driven. As an outcome, we get return on investment and equity. We get a ROAS on touchpoints that we're focused on. We're looking what's up or down versus our blended average profitability. We're asking, 'Are we moving the needle?'

"We are also driving greater attribution of marketing to business growth. Two years ago, a very small percentage of our media was attributed to transactions. Over the last three years, we have been building capability to ensure that eventually all our media will be attributed to behavior. Today, 80% of our digital media is connected to transactions."

At Colgate, ROI is mapped across three levels: media return, shopper lift, and brand equity delta. Its quarterly CMO-CFO sync ensures that marketing is always seen as an investment, not a gamble.

If you want to move hearts, minds, and markets—measure them. Set benchmarks. Share dashboards. Learn from the outliers. Make measurement a shared language across the C-suite.

Eternal Curiosity

More than any framework, any tech stack, or any award, the trait that separates great marketers is this: eternal curiosity. The best marketers lead with diversity of thought—not just marketing books but medical journals, philosophy, AI white papers. Marketing is anthropology in motion. The more you know about people, the better you'll do your job.

"People, creativity, ideas and innovation can change the world," says Haleon's Tamara Rogers. "You need curious people who are empathetic to the audience they're serving, who want to turn insight into actions. In healthcare we look for people who are curious to understand you, and think, as a brand, what can be done to make quality of your life different and better? Some things don't change—it is about what is the unmet need? What is needed here and how can I serve that in a better, more satisfying way?

"Somebody said at a CMO roundtable I was at recently that they feel that marketing and the advertising industry is coming back to being entertaining again. I hope that's true because I think marketing is at its best when teams are having fun, solving problems, being original and innovative."

At Cathay Pacific, curiosity is structured. Its marketers are encouraged to spend hours each month exploring—not benchmarking, not analyzing—just exploring. That's how they caught on to a customer trend: travel ritual videos. It led to an entire user-generated content campaign that performed two times above benchmark.

L'Oréal mandates "cultural safaris"—deep dives into spaces like streetwear, gaming, or Gen Z fragrance rituals. One safari into African grooming culture led to a new line of skin care now sold globally. Curiosity pays.

Shakir Moin's team at Coca-Cola rewatched *Apollo 13* as an exercise in resilience and invention. Not because they're nostalgic but because great marketers learn from everywhere—even space missions.

Curiosity cannot be faked. It must be modeled from the top. If you are not curious, the team won't be either. And curiosity compounds. The more you follow it, the better your instinct becomes. In a world increasingly run by algorithms, curiosity is the most human—and therefore the most powerful—trait you can have in marketing. Stay curious. Stay uncomfortable. That's where the good stuff lives.

"Be open," says Lenovo's Emily Ketchen. "I don't know everything you know. You should be open to questions. Humility opens more doors than authority ever could.

> *"The way you demonstrate the value of the marketing organization is you seek the light and the great examples. I find that if you spend all your time on the troubled spots, it'll sink you. Shine a light; don't chase the shadows."*

Proof in Practice: More Examples of the Six Secrets

The more we look, the more proof we see. These brands aren't lucky. They're intentional. They don't rely on annual campaigns alone—they build marketing operating systems. They embody the six secrets not just in words but in structures, routines, and values.

Marketing isn't just inside their company. It's in their culture.

And that's the goal.

Coca-Cola's Global Playbook: A Lesson in Integration

When Coca-Cola ran its "Taste the Feeling" campaign, it wasn't just a slogan— it was a master class in coordinated global marketing. Behind the scenes, the marketing team had adopted a rigorous internal MaaS structure: a central hub in Atlanta; regional leads in Asia, Latin America, and Europe; and a network of agile agencies. The content wasn't just adapted; it was reverse engineered based on regional insight loops. For example, in Southeast Asia, taste is often tied to cultural gatherings, so the local expressions of the campaign tied Coca-Cola to festivals and family meals. The magic wasn't just the creative—it was the architecture that allowed global consistency with local flavor.

Mastercard and Sonic Branding: Curiosity Turned into Strategy

We're entering an age where visual branding alone is insufficient. Enter sonic branding. Most marketers would run a pitch, pick a jingle, and move on. Mastercard did the opposite. It researched how memory is activated through sound, tested dozens of sound marks in multiple cultural settings, and worked with neurologists to assess subconscious recognition. The result? A globally consistent sonic logo that is used across touchpoints from TV ads to ATMs to event sponsorships. And it came from a simple curiosity: "What if we could be recognized without saying a word?"

Toyota's Campaign Governance System

Toyota's global brand operates like a machine—but with a soul. Its marketing governance system doesn't rely just on KPIs but also a tiered review structure where ideas are judged on feasibility, brand fit, and emotional engagement. One standout success? The "Start Your Impossible" campaign, launched during the Olympics. Born in Japan, it was then localized for twenty-plus countries—with each region contributing storylines featuring local athletes and para-athletes. The original idea was excellent; the system that allowed its global rollout was the secret weapon.

PlayStation and Real-Time Fan Feedback

Sony PlayStation has made feedback loops core to its product marketing cycle. When a new game or feature launches, Reddit threads, Discord groups, and Twitter mentions are monitored live by the community team. During the PlayStation 5 launch, insights from these platforms were fed to the product team and even impacted how they structured inventory updates and feature highlight ads. They even A/B tested trailers based on fan memes and lore references. This is not just data use—it's a cultural immersion strategy.

L'Oréal's Influencer Indexing Model

To measure the real impact of influencer marketing, L'Oréal developed an internal algorithm that scores influencers not just on followers or engagement but on "relevance velocity"—how often they drive actual product consideration within a ten-day period of posting. It pairs this with its own in-house analytics tool to assess conversion lifts in regions like APAC. In India, one such test with micro-influencers resulted in a 43 percent lift in store-search behavior for a hair care product. This rigor comes from a belief that you can't move what you can't measure.

Cathay Pacific's Post-COVID-19 Loyalty Reinvention

Faced with a devastating downturn, Cathay Pacific didn't just reboot its loyalty program—it reimagined what loyalty meant. It introduced "Miles for Moments"—allowing travelers to donate their unused miles to frontline workers or NGOs. It was measured not just in NPS uplift but in earned media, PR value, and reactivation rates. It was a bold bet that compassion could be currency. And it paid off.

Lenovo and Agile War Rooms

In key seasonal marketing moments—like Singles' Day in China or back to school in the United States—Lenovo sets up agile war rooms. These are cross-functional pods where product, creative, data science, and media teams sit together (physically or virtually). Daily stand-ups review campaign performance, and optimizations happen in real time. When one laptop model underperformed in Singapore, the war room adjusted creative, updated product pages, and reallocated budget within forty-eight hours. The sale was saved. MaaS in motion.

Chapter 10
Closing Thoughts:
Looking Forward, Looking Back

In 2013, with the release of my first book, *China CMO*, we thought it would be fun to imagine marketing in China in 2030. We laid out a number of themes—some ambitious, some speculative—and as time has moved on, it's first best to see if they were right.

Back then, we forecast that the China CMO of 2030 would need to be digitally native, culturally fluent, data proficient, and organizationally agile. We talked about innovation and insight. We talked about hypercompetition (it happened!). We talked about marketing for growth. We talked about training talent. We talked about digital changing everything (well, we failed to predict ChatGPT). We talked about improved agency marriages. And we talked about giving back.

The people we interviewed at the time—leaders from Coca-Cola, Lenovo, Mondelēz, IKEA, McDonald's, and others—were already grappling with emerging pressures: localization versus scale, the fragility of brand trust, and the demand to become not just communicators but catalysts for company-wide change.

As 2030 approaches, some of those predictions were more than just accurate—they now feel foundational. Others were outpaced by forces we couldn't have seen coming: the explosion of generative AI, the postpandemic reconfiguration of global consumer priorities, and the emergence of entirely digital-first, values-led challenger brands.

Still, one insight remains constant: The best marketers don't just predict the future. They participate in building it.

Today's most impactful leaders are fluent not only in data and tech but also in empathy, experimentation, and enterprise strategy. Their ability to influence product, policy, and people strategy has never been more vital. They are no longer fighting for a seat at the table—they're building the table.

The final word on the future should fall to the incredible contributors who gave their time for this book. I was often told quite rudely in my career as a consultant that "You spent a lot of time on both sides of the fence—now you're just sitting on it!"—so let's get off the fence and go to ground level for inspiration.

Asmita Dubey of L'Oréal recently said, "We don't see marketing as a function anymore. It's an ecosystem. Creativity, tech, data—they all have to work together in real-time." Her vision reflects the convergence trend we highlighted years ago. At L'Oréal, that convergence is manifested in how beauty tech—AR, AI skin diagnostics, voice commerce—transforms not just consumer engagement but product development itself.

Cheryl Guerin, Executive Vice President at Mastercard, notes, "Brands today must mean something. Priceless is no longer just a campaign—it's a platform for impact." Under Guerin's leadership, Mastercard has embraced inclusive storytelling and created sonic branding strategies that reach far beyond traditional advertising. It's proof that emotional resonance remains the North Star, even in a digital-first age.

Colin Westcott-Pitt at Glanbia reminds us that not all innovation is flashy. "We win when we make health simpler," he shared at a wellness summit. Glanbia's evolution from ingredient company to wellness advocate is a testament to internal transformation—where the role of marketing is just as much internal change management as it is external brand management.

Ed Bell, General Manager of Brand at Cathay Pacific, embraced emotional clarity during the airline's transformation period. "Brand is not what you say. It's how you behave when the chips are down." As Cathay navigated COVID-19 disruptions, Bell's leadership helped frame marketing not as crisis control but as customer clarity.

Emily Ketchen of Lenovo describes her approach as "precision storytelling at global scale." She recognizes that the future belongs to hybrid marketers—those who can blend cultural intelligence with performance muscle. At Lenovo, data doesn't just drive performance—it powers personal relevance, especially in markets where tech adoption is growing fastest.

At **Sony Interactive Entertainment, Eric Lempel** lives where passion meets product. "Gaming is culture," he said. "And culture doesn't stand still." Under his watch, PlayStation has grown beyond hardware into a cultural ecosystem—with content, community, and crossovers that rival Hollywood's.

Mike Tripp, Group Vice President at Toyota North America, puts it simply: "Relevance beats reach." As consumer attention fragments, Toyota's campaigns increasingly revolve around what it calls "cultural docking"— anchoring every initiative in a real human truth. Whether it's Hispanic-owned dealerships or environmental innovation, Tripp's team is making marketing matter in local terms.

Mukul Deoras, former CMO at Colgate-Palmolive, champions global insight powered by local instinct. "Marketing is a language of relevance. Our job is to speak it fluently—everywhere." That belief shows up in Colgate's oral care campaigns, where product, education, and purpose are interwoven in communities from Manila to Mexico City.

Shakir Moin, now leading Coca-Cola North America marketing, speaks often of building "goosebumps moments." But behind that emotion is structure. "You don't need more meetings. You need better marketing rituals," he told his team. Moin's legacy may be how he systematized creative tension, turning marketing into a cultural heartbeat—not a department.

Finally, **Tamara Rogers of Haleon** frames her role as "chief empathy officer." As one of the world's largest health companies, Haleon sits at the intersection of trust, access, and education. Rogers knows that in health, credibility is everything—and her campaigns increasingly center around transparency, inclusivity, and behavioral science.

What Comes Next: The 2035 CMO Revisited

As we look ahead, it's clear that the CMOs of 2035 will be judged not just by what they make but by what they make happen. We're entering an era where they will become chief value officers—responsible not just for brand equity but for cultural equity, employee engagement, and commercial velocity. The marketing team will no longer be a function waiting for briefs but an engine writing the business case for growth.

Take sustainability. By 2035, brands won't be measured simply by their footprint but by their contribution. This means being deeply embedded in environmental, social, and governance reporting; supplier transparency; and product life cycle conversations. As Cheryl Guerin put it, "Brands must do good to be worth anything at all." And marketing, more than any other function, will be responsible for translating intent into impact.

Or consider the role of AI. Already, companies like L'Oréal are experimenting with AI-led creative iterations—Asmita Dubey calls it "human-led, AI-enhanced beauty." The 2035 CMO won't replace creatives with machines, but they will know how to orchestrate teams that include both. AI will take over the grunt work, freeing up more time for brand innovation, empathy design, and experience mapping.

Geography, too, will dissolve. The next generation of marketers won't think in terms of APAC, EMEA, or LATAM. Instead, they will organize around behaviors, psychographics, and movement—understanding how Gen Z in Jakarta and Johannesburg can share the same cultural drivers.

And measurement? It will move beyond vanity. Mukul Deoras's team at Colgate has already built integrated brand performance dashboards—linking oral care behaviors to sales, trust, and access. By 2035, this model will be table stakes. They will be fluent not just in reach and recall but in unit economics, attrition modeling, and brand elasticity scoring.

The structure of marketing teams will change too. We will oversee blended squads—part media, part machine learning, part product design, part community—and the org chart will look more like a neural network than a pyramid. As Emily Ketchen of Lenovo puts it, "The old structure doesn't scale with today's speed. What we need are squads of specialists aligned around moments."

Talent will also be redefined. The best marketers of tomorrow will be hybrids: anthropologists with analytics degrees, poets with coding fluency, designers who can read dashboards. Ed Bell's brand team at Cathay Pacific regularly rotates junior marketers across brand, insights, and operations—to breed flexibility and pattern recognition.

Eric Lempel at PlayStation speaks of marketing as a live organism. "Gaming evolves daily. So should we." This philosophy will define the next generation of leaders. They will build teams that are always learning, always shipping, and always in dialogue with culture.

Even retail is changing. By 2035, commerce will be continuous. Embedded in voice, embedded in experiences, embedded in wearables. Shakir Moin's principle of "goosebumps marketing" will evolve into "ambient storytelling"— where Coca-Cola moments happen without a billboard or a banner. They'll happen in your fridge, your feed, and your fitness tracker.

Tamara Rogers's work at Haleon reminds us that health literacy will be a cornerstone of future brand leadership. As health becomes digitized and personalized, CMOs will need to create not just trust but tools. Education will be a brand's strongest driver of loyalty, especially in categories where misinformation spreads faster than science.

And perhaps the most important shift of all? Measurement will be not just on output but on orchestration.

What did they inspire in their people?

What did they build in their systems?

What did they leave better than they found it?

Final Note

So what does this all add up to? The modern CMO—whether in China, Chile, or Chicago—is no longer defined by where they work but by *how* they work. They are systems thinkers, cultural navigators, and creative scientists. They sit at the intersection of brand, business, and behavior. They must bring inside-out thinking to outside-in problems. The best ones do not operate in functions—they operate in flows. They are connectors, not controllers. Teachers, not just tacticians. They understand that today's marketing is no longer about control but about coherence. And that loyalty is not something you buy—it's something you earn every day.

As we close this book, the question isn't just what the next five years hold. It's "Who are we becoming?"

Marketing will be more autonomous, yes. More immersive. More real time. But the great irony is that as marketing becomes more powered by machines, it must also become *more human.* This book has tried to do something simple: to get inside the modern marketing organization. To understand how it's structured, who drives it, where it wins—and why it fails.

When I was six, I started putting the pieces together in building Airfix kits. All these years later, every leading marketer has to figure out "What are the optimal pieces for me to make marketing magic?" No AI will have that solution.

The next chapter of marketing won't be written in slogans. It will be written in systems. In shared language. In scalable rituals. And those who succeed won't be the loudest or even the most brilliant.

They will be the ones with the courage to lead the long game.

They will be the ones who balance brand and behavior, data and daring, structure and soul.

They will be less about hierarchy and more about influence.

They will be less about campaigns and more about communities.

They will be less about storytelling and more about story living.

And most importantly, they will be the ones asking better questions.

The ones who, like the marketers featured in this book, don't chase the future.

They help create it.

The 2035 CMO isn't coming.

She's already here.

And she's reading this book.

Stay curious. Stay connected. And stay inside the story.

Contributors

- Asmita Dubey, L'Oréal Groupe
- Cheryl Guerin, Mastercard
- Colin Westcott-Pitt, Glanbia Performance Nutrition
- Edward Bell, Cathay Pacific
- Emily Ketchen, Lenovo
- Eric Lempel, Sony Interactive Entertainment
- Michael Tripp, Toyota Motor North America
- Mukul Deoras, Colgate-Palmolive
- Shakir Moin, Coca-Cola North America
- Tamara Rogers, Haleon

Asmita Dubey
Chief Digital and Marketing Officer
L'Oréal Groupe

Asmita Dubey is Chief Digital and Marketing Officer for L'Oréal Groupe, world leader in beauty, with a purpose to "create the beauty that moves the world."

She is steering the L'Oréal Groupe toward augmented marketing with digital and beauty tech at the core.

"At L'Oréal we love to follow the Groupe's mantra 'to seize what is starting.' We are continuously reinventing beauty experiences for the Groupe's 37 global brands driven by purpose, by multi-sensorial journeys in physical, digital and virtual worlds, by using data across business levers and by exploring new frontiers like AI/Gen AI; to drive responsibly the best consumer engagement with beauty.

"This means on one hand we are elevating consumers with new beauty tech services, cracking new codes of beauty in gaming, shifting to new emerging touchpoints, driving a new influence in beauty in a rising creator economy, and leading new channels, while on the other hand we are firmly grounded in scale and deployment, of a data-driven and ROI-based marketing to drive short-term sales as well as to build brand equity in the long term."

Asmita has been awarded the 2023 World Federation of Advertisers Global Marketer of the Year Award and was recognized as number five in the Forbes Most Influential CMOs list.

She is an Indian national with a background in economics and statistics. She began her career in the advertising industry, working in both India and China on campaigns for some of the world's biggest FMCG brands. She joined L'Oréal in 2013 as chief marketing officer for L'Oréal China, where she was responsible for laying the foundations for the Groupe's e-commerce acceleration in China (including building the Groupe's first joint business partnerships with Alibaba and Tencent). Since then she has taken many leadership and transformational roles within the group.

Asmita also serves as a board member of the world's largest consumer healthcare company, Haleon, as an independent nonexecutive director.

Cheryl Guerin
EVP of Global Brand Strategy and Innovation
Mastercard

Cheryl Guerin is Executive Vice President of Global Brand Strategy and Innovation at Mastercard and sits on the company's management committee, a role she has held since 2022. In this capacity, she directs the stewardship and innovation of Mastercard's iconic "Priceless" brand platform and oversees marketing activation across advertising, media, digital, and AI across B2C and B2B audiences.

Guerin has been a driving force behind pioneering initiatives such as the True Name card—awarded a Cannes Lions Grand Prix in 2021—which enables transgender and nonbinary cardholders to display their chosen names. She also launched the Strivers Initiative supporting women and minority small businesses, Priceless Cities experiences, Priceless Surprises, and the Priceless Causes "Stand Up To Cancer" program, which has helped fund seven FDA-approved cancer therapies.

Prior to this, Guerin held senior marketing roles at Mastercard, including leading North America Marketing and Communications, US Marketing, Global Digital Marketing, North America Products and Services, and Global Credit Products. She has been with Mastercard since 2000. Before that, she began her career at Bates, managing campaigns for major consumer and financial brands.

Guerin serves on several boards and industry bodies, including the Advertising Club of New York, Ronald McDonald House NYC, and the Crohn's & Colitis Foundation. She's also a juror for Clio, Effie, and WARC awards. Recognitions include Brand Innovators' Top 100 Women in Brand Marketing, Yahoo Finance's OUTstanding Ally Role Model list, and Women in Payments Change Agent Award.

Colin Westcott-Pitt
Global Chief Brand Officer
Glanbia Performance Nutrition

Colin Westcott-Pitt is a seasoned marketing executive with over twenty-five years of experience in global brand leadership.

Currently serving as Global Chief Brand Officer at Glanbia Performance Nutrition, he oversees renowned brands such as Optimum Nutrition, BSN, and Isopure. Under his leadership, Optimum Nutrition has cemented its position as the world's leading sports nutrition brand, doubling revenue in the last five years and surpassing $1 billion in revenue globally. He played a pivotal role in establishing a partnership between Optimum Nutrition and the McLaren Formula 1 team, aligning the brands' reputation for both high performance and innovation.

Before joining Glanbia, Westcott-Pitt held senior marketing roles at Pernod Ricard and Heineken in the United States and Europe. While at Heineken USA, he led campaigns for brands like Dos Equis, Amstel Light, and Newcastle Brown Ale, including the "Most Interesting Man in the World" campaign for Dos Equis, which significantly boosted the brand's growth and digital engagement. Westcott-Pitt has also completed executive education at INSEAD and Wharton and leads the Marketing Capability program at Glanbia. His strategic approach to brand building and his ability to forge impactful partnerships have solidified his reputation as a leading figure in global marketing.

Edward Bell
GM of Brand, Insights and Marketing Communications
Cathay Pacific

Edward Bell is General Manager of Brand, Insights and Marketing Communications at Cathay Pacific, a role he has held since August 2017. He leads global brand strategy, consumer insights, loyalty marketing, and communications for the Cathay group, encompassing both passenger and cargo businesses.

With nearly three decades of experience in marketing across Asia, Bell began his career in Melbourne before moving into strategic agency roles at Telstra (Sydney) and American Express (Hong Kong) as well as leading positions at Ogilvy Beijing and Mather Shanghai. He later served as head of marketing for Adidas, followed by various leadership roles at Ogilvy and the role of CEO of FCB Greater China prior to joining Cathay Pacific.

Under Bell's leadership, Cathay launched its transformative "Move Beyond" brand platform in 2019, yielding 1.5 billion impressions and boosting brand metrics amid challenging industry conditions. He also spearheaded the merger of Marco Polo Club and Asia Miles into the unified Cathay membership program, achieving 173 percent global membership growth and fifteen campaign impressions. More recently, Bell led the "Feels Good to Move" global campaign and the "We Know How" cargo brand refresh, aligning marketing with emotional storytelling and sustainability initiatives including suitability, acceptability, and feasibility advocacy.

Originally from Melbourne, Bell holds a master's degree in marketing from Melbourne Business School and a bachelor's degree in psychology from La Trobe University. Based in Hong Kong with his wife and three children, he is recognized with IPA and Jay Chiat awards and actively shares his views in industry forums.

Emily Ketchen
SVP and Chief Marketing Officer,
Intelligent Devices Group and International Markets
Lenovo

Emily Ketchen is Senior Vice President and Chief Marketing Officer of the Intelligent Devices Group and International Markets at Lenovo, a role she has held since April 2025. Previously, she was in the same division as a vice president and chief marketing officer, starting in September 2020. She joined the company after nearly nine years at HP. In this position, she leads global brand strategy, customer insights, creative direction, and marketing campaigns across Lenovo's product segments—including PCs, workstations, and smart devices. She also drives geographic growth across EMEA, Asia-Pacific, North America, Latin America, and China.

Prior to Lenovo, Ketchen spent almost a decade at HP in leadership roles such as head of marketing, HP Americas Personal Systems and Marketing Services, and regional head of marketing services for Asia-Pacific/Japan based in Singapore. She also built agency-side experience at Publicis, Grey, McCann Erickson, and others.

A global citizen fluent in Spanish and French, Ketchen holds a degree in international relations from Pitzer College and studied at the Sorbonne and Institut d'Études Politiques in Paris. Based in San Francisco, she is a board member of the Association of National Advertisers. Recognized for leading a data-led, multiyear transformation of Lenovo's marketing function—including forming Centers of Excellence and integrating AI into campaigns—she champions marketing as both creative and growth driven.

Raised as a third-culture kid, Ketchen applies her global upbringing and inclusion mindset to foster innovation—most recently highlighted through the Work for Humankind program addressing Gen Z mental well-being via AI-powered experiences.

Eric Lempel
SVP, Marketing, Sales, Product,
and Business Operations
Sony Interactive Entertainment

Eric Lempel is the Senior Vice President and Head of Global Marketing, Sales, Product and Business Operations at Sony Interactive Entertainment. He drives revenue growth across the company's business verticals. His leadership spans product and data strategy and brand management, including the strategic direction of the PlayStation brand, as well as global media and communications.

Lempel leads data-informed decision-making, focusing on the expanding PlayStation community and delivering compelling customer experiences across all touchpoints, including marketing, sales, products, and services. He directs PlayStation's brand strategy, with a focus on exceeding expectations and fostering emotional connections. The sales organization delivers products and services to the global PlayStation community through a dynamic strategy that includes retail partnerships, PlayStation Direct, and PlayStation Store.

Previously, Lempel served as Senior Vice President of Marketing and Head of PlayStation Network Americas. He led the launch and operations of network services, including PlayStation Store and PlayStation Plus. Under his leadership, the PlayStation Network experienced exponential growth, with PlayStation Store becoming the leading platform for PlayStation game sales.

Since joining the company in 2000, Lempel has held various roles, including leading the Americas launch of PlayStation Network alongside the release of PlayStation 3 in 2006 and the global launch of PlayStation 5 in 2020. Lempel is an industry veteran with more than thirty years of experience. He holds a bachelor of science degree from Hofstra University.

Michael Tripp
Group Vice President of Marketing
Toyota Motor North America

Michael Tripp is Group Vice President of Marketing at Toyota Motor North America, a role he has held since October 2023. In this capacity, he oversees all aspects of Toyota Division advertising, merchandising, media, incentives, analytics, and motorsports—reporting directly to David Christ, Group Vice President and General Manager of Toyota Division in North America.

With nearly three decades at Toyota, Tripp began his career in 1995 as a customer relations representative. He has since held numerous leadership roles across marketing, sales, and regional operations. Notably, he served as Vice President of Vehicle Marketing and Communications for Toyota Division from 2021 to 2023, where he crafted regional marketing strategies, dealer training, and creative asset development.

Tripp also gained global brand experience through his work with Lexus. As General Manager of Lexus Brand Communications and Experience in Europe (Brussels), he supported operations across approximately forty countries, and he helped establish Lexus International's global brand management team in Tokyo as well as strategic communications in Los Angeles.

Prior to joining Toyota, he served six years in the Army National Guard. Tripp holds a master of administration degree from St. Mary's College of California and a bachelor of science degree in industrial psychology and business from Penn State University.

Based in Plano, Texas, he brings a rich blend of customer-focused insight, global brand strategy, and cross-functional leadership to Toyota's North American marketing.

Mukul Deoras
President, Asia-Pacific Division
Colgate-Palmolive

Mukul Deoras is an executive at Colgate-Palmolive, currently serving as President, Asia-Pacific Division, a position he has held since September 2018. With over four decades in fast-moving consumer goods, Mukul began his career at Hindustan Unilever (1984–2004) in progressively senior marketing and sales roles. He joined Colgate-Palmolive in 2004, and over the last two decades he has led the business in Thailand and India and was also Vice President of Global Personal Care Marketing. In 2012, he was elevated to President, Asia Division. In 2015, Mukul assumed the role of Global Chief Marketing Officer, overseeing all global categories, insights, advertising, and shopper marketing until stepping into his current regional leadership.

A graduate of the Indian Institute of Management, Ahmedabad, Mukul is chairman of the board of Colgate-Palmolive (India) Ltd.—a publicly listed company in India—and also serves as an independent director on the board of Wyndham Hotels & Resorts, a NYSE-listed leading global hospitality company. Based in Hong Kong, he brings a rare blend of strategic marketing, P&L leadership, and cross-border operational experience across key markets, including China, India, Southeast Asia, and Australia.

Shakir Moin
President, Marketing
Coca-Cola North America

Shakir Moin is President, Marketing, for Coca-Cola North America. In his current role, he overseas marketing for the entire portfolio of the Coca-Cola Company brands in North America.

Prior to his current role, Shakir was the chief executive officer of Costa Coffee. Shakir was seconded to Costa Coffee from the Coca-Cola Company in July 2019 as chief operating officer. He has worked with the Coca-Cola Company for twenty-seven years and has lived in eleven countries during this time. He served various marketing, general management, commercial, bottling, and strategy roles during his tenure. He moved to Atlanta, Georgia, in 2017 and was appointed Chief of Staff and Head of Global Growth Operations, reporting to the chief growth officer of the Coca-Cola Company.

Prior to his US-based stint, Shakir served as Chief Marketing Officer for Coca-Cola China, where he was able to establish Coca-Cola marketing as the most admired among more than seventy global and local brands. Shakir also carries the rare experience of developing and executing a launch campaign for Coca-Cola in a totally new Coca-Cola market, Myanmar, in 2013.

Shakir has led every one of his assignments with the ethos that "great people build great brands" and always makes people and marketing capability his primary objective, with a global view of delivering world-class marketing.

In 2024, Shakir was recognized by *Forbes* as one of the Entrepreneurial CMO 50 in North America. In the same year, Shakir was also recognized by Gold House as one of the 100 Most Impactful Asian Pacific Leaders. In 2023 and 2024, Shakir was selected by Campaign USA in its Annual CMO 50 list recognizing the most "intrepid and culture-making brand marketers." Shakir was also recognized as one of the 50 Most Outstanding Asians in America by Asian American Development Center in the same year. He has been awarded the Coca-Cola Marketing Excellence Award twice and was also recognized with the Asian Super Achiever Award by CMO Asia in 2010.

He lives in Atlanta with his wife and two children.

Tamara Rogers
Chief Marketing Officer
Haleon

Tamara Rogers is Chief Marketing Officer at Haleon, a position she has held since July 2022 after being appointed earlier at GSK's consumer healthcare division in 2018. With over thirty years of experience in fast-moving consumer goods, she began her career at Unilever in 1993 as a management trainee in the United Kingdom and rose through roles, including Executive Vice President, Global Deodorants, and Executive Vice President, Personal Care North America, over her nearly twenty-five-year tenure.

At Haleon, she spearheaded the corporate branding strategy to create the identity and purpose of the July 2022 spin-off and established marketing as a central growth function, driving innovation and championing digital integration. She leads marketing teams around the world focused on building superior brands such as Sensodyne, Panadol, Centrum, and Otrivin, with a focus on lifting health inclusivity with purpose-driven campaigns like #ListenToPain and Advil's Pain Equity Project. The company has achieved market share gains, most recently hitting 71 percent of business, winning or holding share across categories.

A board member of the Global Self-Care Federation, Rogers was also appointed an independent nonexecutive director at Greggs effective June 1, 2024, serving on its audit, remuneration, and nominations committees.

Born in Zambia and based in the United Kingdom, Rogers is educated in the sciences and brings a global mindset, P&L expertise, and a proven record in operational and cross-market leadership, especially across EMEA and North America.

References

Chapter 1
The Evolution of the Marketing Organization

"Mattel's Marketing Makeover: How CMO Lisa McKnight Helped Reinvent Barbie." *Ad Age*, May 9, 2022. https://adage.com/article/cmo-strategy/mattel-cmo-lisa-mcknight-barbie-marketing-strategy/2413241.

"Disney's Reorganization Puts Streaming at the Center of Its Business." Bloomberg, October 12, 2020. https://www.bloomberg.com/news/articles/2020-10-12/disney-reorganizes-media-and-entertainment-business.

"How Mattel Turned Barbie into a Billion-Dollar Brand Again." CNBC, July 19, 2023. https://www.cnbc.com/2023/07/19/how-mattel-turned-barbie-into-a-billion-dollar-brand-again.html.

"Why Ferrar's New CEO Is Prioritizing Brand and Customer Experience." *Fast Company*, March 25, 2021. https://www.fastcompany.com/90617437/ferrari-ceo-brand-customer-experience.

"How Mattel Rebuilt Its Brand." *Harvard Business Review*, November 2021. https://hbr.org/2021/11/how-mattel-rebuilt-its-brand.

"Netflix Names Marian Lee as New Chief Marketing Officer." *Hollywood Reporter*, February 9, 2023. https://www.hollywoodreporter.com/business/business-news/netflix-names-new-cmo-marian-lee-1235318662/.

References

"Barbie's Marketing Machine: How Warner Bros. and Mattel Create a Cultural Event." *Variety*, July 18, 2023. https://variety.com/2023/film/news/barbie-marketing-campaign-warner-bros-mattel-1235674564/.

"How Coca-Cola Is Transforming Its Marketing Strategy." *Wall Street Journal*, November 8, 2021. https://www.wsj.com/articles/coca-cola-marketing-strategy-transformation-11636384201.

Chapter 2

How Marketing Decisions Get Made

Airbnb. *Form S-1 Registration Statement.* US Securities and Exchange Commission, 2020. https://www.sec.gov/Archives/edgar/data/1559720/000119312520303821/d87104ds1.htm.

Airbnb. *Annual Report 2022.* https://investors.airbnb.com/.

Discuss.io. *How Haleon Is Radically Transforming Consumer Understanding with Discuss.* 2022. https://www.discuss.io/customer-stories/how-haleon-is-radically-transforming-consumer-understanding-with-discuss/.

Deloitte. *The CMO Survey: Marketing Transformation at Microsoft.* 2021. https://www2.deloitte.com/us/en/pages/chief-marketing-officer/articles/microsoft-cmo-survey.html.

Microsoft. *Annual Report 2023.* https://www.microsoft.com/investor/reports/ar23/index.html.

Nestlé. *Creating Shared Value and Sustainability Report 2021.* 2022. https://www.nestle.com/sites/default/files/2022-03/nestle-csv-sustainability-report-2021-en.pdf.

Sweney, M. "How Airbnb Changed Its Marketing Strategy During the Pandemic." *The Guardian*, March 8, 2021. https://www.theguardian.com/business/2021/mar/08/how-airbnb-changed-its-marketing-strategy-during-the-pandemic.

Chapter 3

The Shape of Marketing Teams

"How Adidas Uses Agile to Move Faster in Digital Marketing." AdExchanger, March 2, 2020. https://www.adexchanger.com/commerce/

how-adidas-uses-agile-to-move-faster-in-digital-marketing/.

Adidas AG. *Annual Report 2023*. https://report.adidas-group.com/2023/en/.

Business Model Navigator. *Royal Philips Business Model*. N.d. https://www.businessmodelnavigator.com/case-firm?id=114.

Cathay Pacific. *Cathay and Publicis Groupe Hong Kong Launch "Feels Good to Move" Brand Campaign*. March 1, 2023. https://www.cathaypacific.com/cx/en_HK/about-us/press-room/press-release/2023/cathay-and-publicis-groupe-hong-kong-launch-feels-good-to-move-brand-campaign.html.

Cape. *How Cathay Pacific Localizes Ads in 13 Languages for 32 Markets*. 2023. https://www.cape.io/cases/cathay-pacific.

Choudhury, V., and R. Sabherwal. "Portfolios of Control in Outsourced Software Development Projects." *Information Systems Research* 14(3) (2003): 291–314.

"How Gore's Unique Culture Drives Innovation." *Forbes*, June 17, 2019. https://www.forbes.com/sites/forbeshumanresourcescouncil/2019/06/17/how-gores-unique-culture-drives-innovation/.

"Agile Transformation at Adidas: Scaling Up and Staying Customer-Obsessed." *Forbes*, January 27, 2020. https://www.forbes.com/sites/stevedenning/2020/01/27/agile-transformation-at-adidas-scaling-up-and-staying-customer-obsessed/.

Gartner. *2022 Marketing Organization Survey*. https://www.gartner.com/en/insights/marketing.

Gartner. *CMO Strategic Priorities Survey*. 2024. https://www.gartner.com/en/articles/marketers-are-under-pressure-to-adapt-quickly-in-2024.

IBM. *Integrated Report 2023*. https://www.ibm.com/investor/annual-report.

L'Oréal. *Universal Registration Document 2022*. https://www.loreal-finance.com/en/annual-report-2022/.

Procter & Gamble. *Annual Report 2022*. https://us.pg.com/investors/annual-report/.

Royal Philips. *Annual Report 2022*. https://www.results.philips.com/publications/ar22/downloads/pdf/en/PhilipsFullAnnualReport2022-English.pdf.

Chapter 4
The CMO as Growth Architect

Back to Front Show. *Who Owns e.l.f. Cosmetics? The Surprising Story Behind the Brand.* 2024. https://www.backtofrontshow.com/elf-cosmetics-brand-story/.

"How Oreo and Ritz Maker Mondelez Is Trying to Stay Relevant by Funding Startups and New Product Lines in Areas Like Prebiotic and Paleo Food." Business Insider, January 13, 2020.

Evolut Agency. *The e.l.f. Beauty Marketing Blueprint—Key Lessons in 2022.* 2022. https://evolut.agency/elf-beauty-marketing-case-study/.

"GSK's Consumer Healthcare Business Rebrands as Haleon Ahead of Spin-Off." *Forbes*, February 22, 2022. https://www.forbes.com/sites/forbescommunicationscouncil/2022/02/22/gsk-rebrands-as-haleon-ahead-of-spin-off/.

Glossy. *e.l.f.'s TikTok Strategy: Make Viral Songs That Slap.* December 16, 2019. https://www.glossy.co/beauty/e-l-f-s-tiktok-strategy-make-viral-songs-that-slap/.

"'Fast and Cheap': How AB InBev Is Driving Innovation." *Marketing Week*, July 24, 2019. https://www.marketingweek.com/ab-inbev-innovation-fast-cheap/.

"Haleon Unveils Brand-Driven Growth Strategy Ahead of GSK Split." *Marketing Week*, February 22, 2022. https://www.marketingweek.com/haleon-growth-strategy-gsk/.

"Interview: The Making of Haleon Following Its Demerger from GSK: Tamara Rogers." Marketing Interactive, 2022. https://www.marketing-interactive.com/haleon-tamara-rogers-interview-demerge-gsk.

Mondelez International. "Martin Renaud Wins Coveted CMO Award: Recognition for Marketing Team's Data-Driven Approach" (press release). August 4, 2022.

Mondelez International. "Mondelez International Releases Fifth Annual State of Snacking Report; Dirk Van de Put and Martin Renaud Comment" (press release). *Deli Market News*, March 18, 2024.

Shorty Awards. *e.l.f. Cosmetics: Eyes. Lips. Face.* 2020. https://shortyawards.com/12th/eyes-lips-face.

VentureFuel. "Brewing Up the Future—Pedro Earp, CMO AB InBev &

Head of ZX Ventures." Podcast. 2021. https://venturefuel.net/podcast/pedro-earp-ab-inbev/.

World Federation of Advertisers. "Interview: Martin Renaud, EVP & Chief Marketing and Sales Officer, Mondelez International" (YouTube video). N.d.

Chapter 5
Finding, Keeping, and Nurturing Top Marketing Talent

Kraft Heinz. "Inside the Kitchen: How Kraft Heinz Is In-Housing Creativity." *Marketing Dive*, 2021. https://www.marketingdive.com/news/kraft-heinz-in-house-agency-the-kitchen/.

LinkedIn. *Workforce Report—U.S.* 2023. https://economicgraph.linkedin.com/resources/linkedin-workforce-report.

L'Oréal. "How L'Oréal Became a Beauty Tech Powerhouse." *Harvard Business Review* (digital article), 2021. https://hbr.org/2021/05/how-loreal-became-a-beauty-tech-powerhouse.

"Career and Salary Survey 2023." *Marketing Week,* 2023. https://www.marketingweek.com/career-and-salary-survey-2023/.

Statista. *Marketing Manager Employment Outlook in the U.S. 2022–2032.* https://www.statista.com/statistics/1255434/us-marketing-manager-job-growth/.

World Federation of Advertisers. *Global Talent Crisis Survey.* 2022. https://wfanet.org/knowledge/item/2022/09/06/The-Marketing-Talent-Crisis-WFA-Report.

Chapter 6
Marketing Outside: Working with Agencies

Colgate-Palmolive. *RedFuse: A Bespoke Agency Solution.* N.d. https://www.colgatepalmolive.com.

Dentsu Group Inc. *Integrated Growth Solutions and Global Transformation.* 2023. https://www.group.dentsu.com.

Interpublic Group. *Acxiom and Data-Driven Marketing Evolution.* 2022. https://www.interpublic.com.

Mastercard. *Priceless Campaign History.* N.d. https://www.mastercard.com/global/

en/vision/corporate-responsibility/priceless.html.

McCann Worldgroup. *Mastercard Case Studies and Global Campaigns*. N.d. https://www.mccannworldgroup.com.

Publicis Groupe. *Power of One: A Connected Model*. 2023. https://www.publicis-groupe.com.

Saatchi & Saatchi. *Toyota and Saatchi Partnership History*. N.d. https://www.saatchi.com.

Team One USA. *Our Work with Lexus*. N.d. https://www.teamone-usa.com.

Toyota Motor North America. *Agency Partnerships and Brand Architecture*. 2023. https://www.pressroom.toyota.com.

WPP. *Company Transformation and Agency Consolidation Strategy*. 2022. https://www.wpp.com.

Chapter 7
Tools of the Trade: Marketing's Other Muscle

Adobe. *Customer Success Story: Adobe's Own Digital Transformation*. N.d. https://business.adobe.com.

Bayer. *Bayer Brings Media Buying In-House with New Operating Model*. 2022. https://www.marketingweek.com/bayer-in-housing-model/.

Digiday. *Bayer Saved at Least $10 Million After Taking Programmatic In-House*. 2019. Retrieved from Digiday website.

CxO Institute. *Glanbia Case Study*. July 2023. Retrieved from CxO Institute website.

Gartner. *Magic Quadrant for Multichannel Marketing Hubs*. 2023. https://www.gartner.com/en/research/magic-quadrant.

"How to Build a Marketing Tech Stack That Works." *Harvard Business Review*, 2020. https://hbr.org.

Latterly. *Sony PlayStation Marketing Strategy 2025: A Case Study*. Latterly.org. 2024. Retrieved from Latterly website.

McKinsey & Company. *Marketing's New Mandate: Building the Modern Marketing Operating Model*. 2022. https://www.mckinsey.com/business-functions/growth-marketing-and-sales/our-insights/marketings-new-mandate.

Monks. *Data and Media Transformation & In-Housing Support Case | Bayer*. N.d. Retrieved from Monks website.

Salesforce. *State of Marketing: 8th Edition*. 2023. https://www.salesforce.com/resources/research-reports/state-of-marketing/.

SEINō. "Case Study: Glanbia Real-Time Email Tracking and Reporting" (blog post). 2024. Retrieved from SEINō website.

Schultz, D. E., C. H. Patti, and P. J. Kitchen. *The Evolution of Integrated Marketing Communications: The Customer-Driven Marketplace*. Routledge, 2013.

WARC Opinion. *Bayer Sees Benefits from In-Housing Media*. 2019. Retrieved from WARC website.

Westcott, M., and G. Dixon. *Reimagining the marketing operating model*. Deloitte Insights, 2021. https://www2.deloitte.com.

Chapter 8
Performance Management: Driving Accountability and Results

AB InBev. *draftLine Performance Framework Overview* (internal case summary). 2022.

Lob. *Precision, Profit, and Predictive Analytics in Direct Mail* (blog post). 2023. https://www.lob.com/blog/how-predictive-analytics-supercharges-direct-mail-campaigns.

MediaSense and World Federation of Advertisers. *Three-Quarters of Brands Want to Change Their Agency Remuneration Model*. World Federation of Advertisers, November 14, 2024. https://wfanet.org/knowledge/item/2024/11/14/three-quarters-of-brands-want-to-change-their-agency-remuneration-model/.

System1. *Creative Consistency: How Sustained Creative Partnerships Drive Profit* (white paper). 2020.

Toyota Australia. "Standard Agency Review Confirms Saatchi & Saatchi as Lead Retail Partner" (press release). 2024.

WARC. *Unilever: Driving Performance Management Through Pay-for-Performance* [Case study]. WARC. Ad Age. March 12, 2009. Unilever's bold move to performance-based agency contracts. *Advertising Age*.

Chapter 9
The Six Secrets to Great Marketing

Business of Fashion. *How L'Oréal Measures Influencer Marketing Success.* May 17, 2021. https://www.businessoffashion.com/articles/news-bites/how-loreal-measures-influencer-marketing-success/.

Cathay Pacific. *Miles for Good—Making a Difference.* July 7, 2020. https://news.cathaypacific.com/miles-for-good-making-a-difference.

L'Oréal Group. *Driving Digital Excellence Through Beauty Tech.* October 2020. https://www.loreal.com/en/articles/digital/digital-transformation-beauty-tech/.

Lenovo StoryHub. *How Lenovo Innovated for Singles' Day 2020.* November 13, 2020. https://news.lenovo.com/news/how-lenovo-innovated-for-singles-day-2020/.

Mastercard. *Mastercard Launches Sonic Brand.* February 8, 2019. https://www.mastercard.com/news/perspectives/2019/mastercard-launches-sonic-brand/.

Rajamannar, R. *Quantum Marketing: Mastering the New Marketing Mindset for Tomorrow's Consumers.* HarperCollins Leadership, 2021.

Takahashi, D. *How Sony Designed the PlayStation 5 Interface.* VentureBeat, November 12, 2020. https://venturebeat.com/games/how-sony-designed-the-playstation-5-interface/.

Coca-Cola Company. *Coca-Cola Launches "One Brand" Global Marketing Strategy.* January 19, 2016. https://www.coca-colacompany.com/news/coca-cola-launches-one-brand-global-marketing-strategy.

Toyota Motor Corporation. *Toyota Launches Global "Start Your Impossible" Campaign.* February 9, 2018. https://global.toyota/en/newsroom/corporate/21122234.html.